AF574403

Paul Gauguin

Paul Gauguin

Stephen F. Eisenman

Photographic credits:

Aargauer Kunsthaus, Aarau, Switzerland (p.13); Albright-Knox Art Gallery, Buffalo, New York (pp. 40, 54); Ateneum Art Museum, Helsinki (p. 88); Baltimore Museum of Art, Baltimore (pp. 61, 67); Bayerische Staatsgemäldesammlungen, Neue Pinakothek, Munich (p. 71); Colección Thyssen-Bornemisza, Madrid (p. 59); Courtauld Institute Galleries, London (pp. 73, 74); Hammer Museum, Los Angeles (p. 31); Honolulu Academy of Arts, Hawaii (p. 56); Kunstmuseum, Basel (p. 91); Kunsthaus, Switzerland (p. 22); Museu de Arte, São Paulo (p. 72); Museum Folkwang, Essen (pp. 35, 90); Museo Nacional de Bellas Artes, Buenos Aires (pp. 17, 62); Musée d'Orsay, Paris (pp. 32, 37, 38, 46, 53); Museum of Fine Arts, Boston (pp. 76- 77); Nasjonalgalleriet, Oslo (p. 11); National Gallery of Art, Washington (pp. 6, 16, 23, 43, 57, 75, 78); National Gallery of Scotland, Edinburgh (p. 27); National Galleries of Scotland, Edinburgh (p. 82); Norton Gallery of Art, West Palm Beach (p. 41); Ny Carlsberg Glyptotek, Copenhagen (p. 14); National Museum of Western Art, Tokyo (p. 36); Ohara Museum of Art, Kurashiki (p. 63); Ordrupgaard Museum, Copenhagen (pp. 8, 24, 28); Private Collection (pp. 39, 65, 66); Private Collection, Berne (p. 15); Private Collection, Cleveland (p.19); Private Collection, New York (p.18); Private Collection, Zurich (p. 86); Rijksmuseum Vincent van Gogh, Amsterdam (pp. 33, 69); Rudolf Staechelin Foundation, Switzerland (p. 60); Sterling and Francine Clark Art Institute, Williamstown, Massachusetts (p. 70); The Art Institute of Chicago, Chicago (pp.34, 68); The Chrysler Museum, Norfolk (p. 42); The Cleveland Museum of Art, Cleveland (pp. 44, 87); The Metropolitan Museum of Art, New York (pp. 49, 79); The State Hermitage, St. Petersburg (pp. 58, 83, 84); The Museum of Modern Art, New York (p. 64); Tate Gallery, London (pp. 80-81); Van Gogh Museum, Amsterdam (pp. 20, 21, 30); Worcester Art Museum, Massachusetts (p. 50).

Balmes, 54. 08007 Barcelona (Spain)
www.edicionespoligrafa.com

Coordination: Aymara Arreaza
Text: Stephen F. Eisenman
Proofreading: Sol García Galland
Translation: Guillermina Rosenkrantz, pp. 92-93
Design: makingbooks / Carlos J. Santos
Color separation: Estudi Polígrafa / Annel Biu
Printing and binding: Abacus Gráfica, Valencia

Available in USA and Canada through D.A.P./Distributed Art Publishers
155 Sixth Avenue, 2nd Floor, New York, N.Y. 10013
Tel. (212) 627-1999 Fax: (212) 627-9484

ISBN: 978-84-343-1249-4
Dep. legal: B. 33.704-2010 (Printed in Spain)

Contents

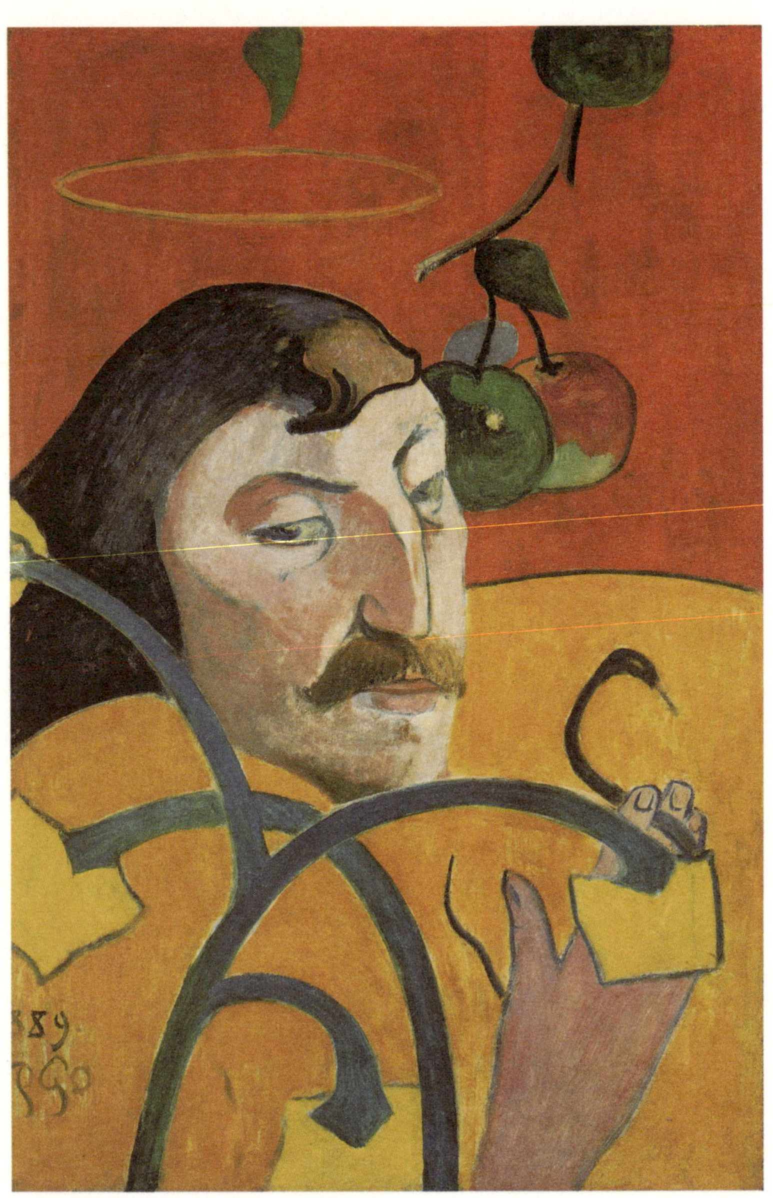

Portrait of Gauguin by Himself,
1889.
Oil on wood, 79.6 × 51.7 cm.
National Gallery of Art,
Washington.

Stephen F. Eisenman Gauguin's Dream of a Golden Age

Introduction: Gauguin and Greco-Roman Antiquity. Among the splendors of ancient Greece and Rome—less monumental than the Parthenon and Coliseum but just as long lasting—are its myths and dreams of a golden age. These ancient figures of thought, which invoke imagined, and still more remote times and places where there was perfect easefulness and plenty, first appear in the poetry of Hesiod from the late 8th century BC. In his *Works and Days*, sometimes described as the earliest Western study of economics and labor, Hesiod described the present Iron Age as one of discord, misery and ceaseless toil. But, he sings, it was not always thus. In the Golden Age, people "lived as if they were gods, their hearts free from all sorrow,/by themselves, and without hard work or pain; no miserable/old age came their way; their hands, their feet, did not alter...[and] when they died, it was as if they fell asleep."[1]

In the texts of the 5th century BC Empedocles too, which we know chiefly from the writings of Plato and Aristotle, as well as from a few Egyptian papyrus fragments, humans once lived in a golden age free of violence and strife, under the guidance of Aphrodite, goddess of love and sex. Even sacrifices to the gods were forbidden in this period, as well as the eating of animal flesh. Because animals may be reincarnated as humans, to kill and eat one is murder and cannibalism.

In the poetry and prose of Ovid, Virgil, and other Roman authors, and in Roman wall painting and sculpture, the ancient myth of a golden age received its fullest accounting. The idealized epoch was now not simply a lost past, but a realizable present and future. In Virgil's *Fourth Eclogue*, the poet described the end of the Iron Age of warfare and want, and the beginning of a Golden Age of peace and pleasure, when labor, even including artistic and craft labor, would cease, as nature itself came to resemble art: "The ground will not suffer the mattock, nor the vine the pruning hook; now likewise the strong ploughman shall loose his bulls from the yoke. Neither shall wool learn to counterfeit changing hues, but the ram in the meadow shall dye his fleece now with soft glowing sea-purple, now with yellow saffron; native scarlet shall clothe the lambs at their pasturage."[2] Like the late-medieval English "Land of Cockaigne," or the Renaissance "greene cabinet" of Spenser's last eclogue from *The Shepheards Calender*, the Roman Arcadia is a place where the earth freely yields its harvests, beauty never fades, and death is notable only because of its great rarity. When fair Daphnis is slain, Virgil writes in the *Fifth Eclogue*, the Punic lions mourn his passing, and the "large barley" cedes to "fruitless darnel and barren wild oats."[3] Even in Arcadia, there is death (*et in Arcadia ego*), but it is just the shadow of a cloud passing above an otherwise perpetually sun washed landscape.

• • •

1 *Hesiod, The Works and Days/Theogony/The Shield of Herakles,* translated by Richard Lattimore. Ann Arbor: University of Michigan Press, 1959, pp. 31-43.

2 Virgil, *The Eclogues,* translated by J.W. Mackail. Portland, Maine: Thomas B. Mosher, 1898, pp. 35-36.

3 Ibid, p. 44.

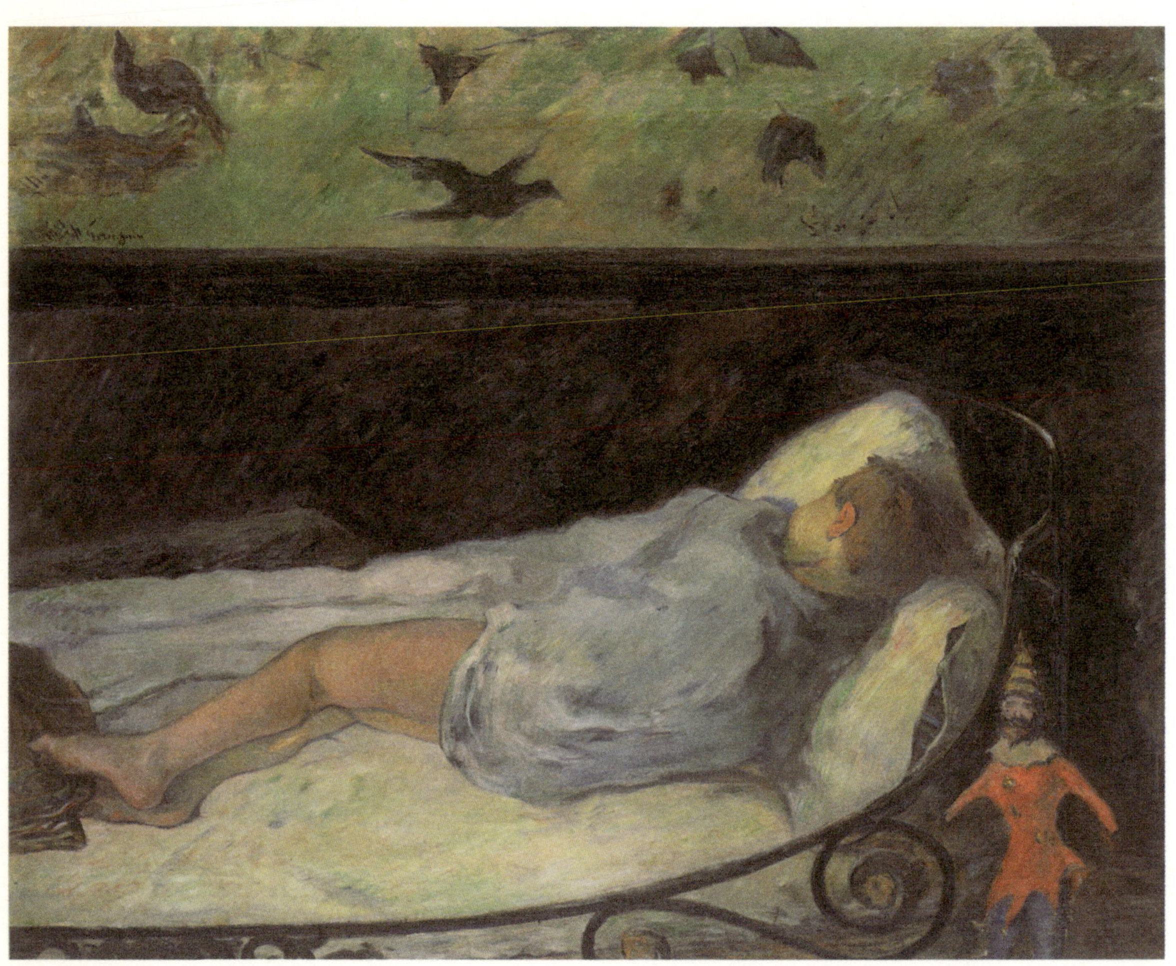

The Little One is Dreaming,
Étude, 1881.
Oil on canvas, 59.5 × 73.5 cm.
Ordrupgaard Museum,
Copenhagen.

Roman wall paintings from the *Villa of P. Fannius Synistor* at Boscoreale, (c. 40–30 BC), and from *The House of Livia* at Primaporta (c. 30-40 BC), depict a mythic, pastoral and Dionysian landscape in which architecture, fertile fields, marble sculptures, birds, flowers and animals freely intermingle. All distinctions between city and country are erased, and Gods disport with mortals. In the great *Ara Pacis* of Caesar Augustus from 13 BC, allegorical figures of Earth, Air and Water symbolize the fertility of Italy under the beneficent order of the *Pax Romana*. The altar was erected on the Field of Mars, in a sacred grove; its architecture and sculpture harkens back to Hellenistic Greek monuments, and thus again to an idealized golden age of peace and abundance.

This ancient, utopian tradition, the beautiful dream of poets and artists living in territories dependent for their prosperity upon cruel warfare and pitiless slavery, long outlived the decline and fall of the Roman Empire itself. It survived as a balm for cultures and societies themselves marked by violence, poverty and exploitation, and as a compass for revolutionists who wanted to change everything. Nearly two millennia after Virgil, it became enmeshed in the culture of modernity and central to the art and thought of Paul Gauguin. From Édouard Manet to Piet Mondrian, as the American critic Clement Greenberg wrote in 1946: "What characterizes painting...is its pastoral mood...the preoccupation with nature at rest, human beings at leisure, and art in movement." Avant-garde art was pastoral, the critic wrote, because it was the product of a deep dissatisfaction with modernity, and hope a redeemed future.[4] For the French artist Gauguin, immured in modern Paris, heartily sick of the daily struggle for survival in a country that was itself a rapacious Empire, myths of a surviving, primitive culture in Martinique, Brittany and Arles, and dreams of a free life among the peaceful inhabitants of Oceania were a liberation; they fired his imagination and sustained his artistic energies. In 1891, on the eve of his move to the South Pacific, Gauguin invoked the metaphorical language of Virgil when he described his hope of finding an Arcadian realm, "of ecstasy, peace and art, far from this European struggle for money."

Gauguin found both less, and more than he bargained for in Tahiti; the primitive order of which he dreamed was ended, if it ever existed. But the richness and complexity of the life he saw at times overwhelmed him; it nevertheless stimulated the growth of one of the most vivid and sustained bodies of work in the history of art. No artist, before or since, has so assiduously considered and recorded—albeit in symbolic form—the encounter between a European colonist and native subjects, nor so thoroughly transformed this fraught relation into pictorial myths concerned with temptation, desire, frustration and loss. Gauguin, the dreamer of dreams, and Gauguin the Symbolist, was also Gauguin the Virgilian and Gauguin the classicist, whose patterns of thinking were dependent upon some of the artistic and literary traditions of ancient Greece and Rome. Gauguin was at the same time a kind of uncertain and posturing Odysseus, wandering the seas, living a life of adventure as well as privation, and longing for a return to the sanctuary and shelter of friends and family. Unlike Odysseus, however, he could not resist the Sirens' song, and died an exile, 6,000 miles from home.

Gauguin was clearly not a conventional classicist, (even less an Academic), or a Homeric hero. His golden age was not that of Alexandre Cabanel or W.A. Bouguereau, who painted paper mache Venuses floating on cardboard seas. Nor was it even that of Camille Corot, painter of wood nymphs and endless dawns, or Pierre Puvis de Chavannes, artist of sacred groves and Mount Parnassus. Certainly, Gauguin greatly admired these last two artists, and wrote in a letter to his friend Schuffenecker that, "Corot's entire soul has passed through his landscapes; the air breathes good-

• • •

4 Clement Greenberg, *Collected Essays and Criticism*. Chicago: University of Chicago Press, 1986, vol. 2, pp. 51-52.

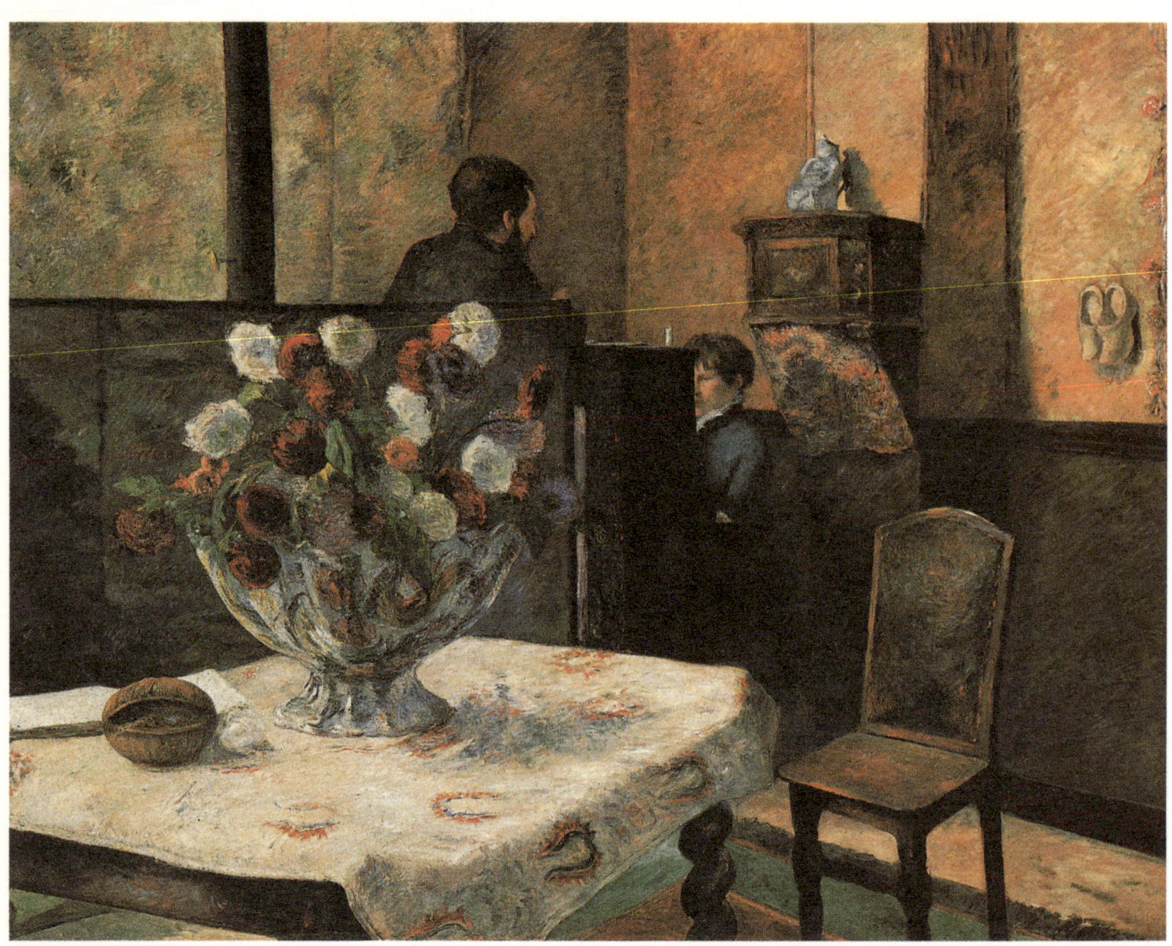

Interior of the Artist's Home,
1881.
Oil on canvas, 130.5 × 162.5 cm.
Nasjonalgalleriet, Oslo.

ness, while the slender tree trunks express grace and nobility."[5] Puvis' influence too is pervasive, especially in scenes of bathers, and Gauguin openly acknowledged the debt. But unlike these artist's works, Gauguin's are often purposely awkward, or what he called *savage*. His landscapes are sometimes indecipherable, with planes colliding with planes, and strange forms appearing with little foundation in nature, such as the polyhedron at the upper right of the *Young Breton Bathers* (1888), or the melted bodies and odd pattern of ripples and reflections in *The Geese* (1889) that suggest nothing so much as the dreamscapes of Salvador Dalí or Yves Tanguy. (No matter that there is an objective correlative for the latter scene—plants, animals and people seen in reflection on the surface of water—the picture remains phantasmagoric.) In addition, many of Gauguin's figures are ungainly —*laid* (ugly) in the blunt language of the French art criticism of the day. His native women—dark complexioned and thick limbed with big feet, such as in *Te Avae No Maria* (*The Month of Mary,* 1899)—don't look like Venus. And his men—gangly, lumbering and often expressionless, such as his *Poor Fisherman,* (1896)—don't resemble Odysseus, Achilles or Agamenon. But Gauguin undoubtedly drew upon his knowledge of the myths and tales of ancient gods and heroes when he painted his Breton, Martinique, Tahitian and finally Marquesan subjects. They possess a prepossession quite unlike that found in previous representations of indigenous people, (for example the Indians portrayed by the American George Catlin), and an authority that appears, at times, Olympian, as in *Te pape nave nave* (*Delectable Waters*, 1898, p. 78), or *Tahitian Woman* (1898), with its derivation from the figure of Dionysos from the east pediment of the Parthenon.
Of course, such references to classical antiquity may seem inevitable. At an historical moment when ethnological research and understanding of so-called "primitive cultures"—the cultures of non-European foragers, pastoralists, horticulturalists and other relatively egalitarian, native communities—was in its infancy, Gauguin could not envision indigenous society in Martinique or the South Pacific without some recourse to ancient Greek, Roman, Virgilian and Golden Age paradigms. But the extent of Gauguin's engagement with antiquity is more than simply instinctive. He referred to Virgil in several letters and other writings, and derived a number of compositions from photographs of ancient, Roman monuments. For example, many of the artist's late representations of horses and riders, or horses and standing attendants, including *Faiara* (*The Awakening*, 1898) and the woodcut *Maruru* (*Thanks,* 1893), were derived from details visible on the lower southwest sections of Trajan's Column. Gauguin owned at least two collotypes of the column, made and published by his former guardian, Gustave Arosa.[6] In other works, for example *The Call* (1902, p. 87), *The Invocation* (1903), and *Marquesan Man in a Red Cape* (1902), Gauguin included a pair of mysterious, caped figures, joined at the hip, obviously derived from the type of Dante and Virgil, famously represented by Eugène Delacroix in *The Barque of Dante* (1823) and by Gustave Doré in his wood engraved illustrations for Dante's *The Divine Comedy*. As much as to France and the Pacific therefore, Gauguin belongs to Rome and the classical tradition.

Utopians in the Family. Gauguin was born in Paris in 1848 but lived the first seven years of his life in Lima, Peru. The artist's parents, Clovis Gauguin and Aline Chazal, were committed republicans—she was the daughter of the great utopian-socialist, Flora Tristan (1803–1844)—and fled France in August, 1849 in anticipation of the coming Empire. From Aline, and from

• • •

5 Paul Gauguin, *Correspondence de Paul Gauguin*, edited by Victor Merlhés. Paris: Foundation Singer-Polignac, 1984, vol. 1, p. 306; cited in Guillermo Solana, "The Faun Awakes. Gauguin and the Revival of the Pastoral," *Gauguin and the Origins of Symbolism*. Madrid: Fundación Colección Thyssen-Bornemisza, 2005, p. 20.

6 Wilhelm Froehner, *La Colonne Trajane, interprétée par…Reproduction en gravure phototypique par Gustave Arosa*, 3 vols. Paris, 1870; also: Wilhelm Froehner, *La Colonne Trajane*…5 vols. Paris, 1872-74. Gauguin owned plates 29 and 98. The photographs were acquired by Victor Segalen at the 1903 auction of the deceased artist's possessions, and passed into the collection of his daughter, Mme. A Joly-Segalen. See: William M. Kane, "Gauguin's Cheval Blanc: Sources and Syncretic Meanings," *The Burlington Magazine*, vol. 180 (760), July 1966, p. 356.

books, Gauguin learned of his maternal grandmother's feelings of revulsion toward the bourgeoisie of her day, and dreams that the world might one day "offer [itself as] a huge and magnificent garden for everyone, that humanity might become a great and unified family of which each member should live as they chose and receive each according to their needs."[7] Though completely disdainful of the institutions, dogmas, and traditions of the Catholic Church, Tristan was nevertheless convinced that the lessons of primitive Christianity—love, charity and equality—remained salient in the modern age. Gauguin much later expressed some similar ideas in his "The Modern Spirit and Catholicism," and other writings.

Gauguin's early years in Peru, although spent in the confines of family and local elites, nevertheless allowed the adult artist to claim an exotic identity, aspects of which would appear and reappear in chameleon-like self-portraits, including *Bonjour M. Gauguin* (1889), where he wore the garb of a Breton pilgrim. An alternative, exotic identity is visible in the drawing *Ia Orana Ritou* (c.1892), where he depicted himself as an indigenous Tahitian, draped in a *pareu*, (a wrap-around skirt), about to begin his day's work; and in the great, Rembrandt-like *Self-Portrait* (1896, p. 72) in which—standing in front of a large, exotic carving of his own—he wears a mask-like expression above his thick body covered in a thin, white chemise.

After a period of education in Orléans and Paris, Gauguin entered the merchant marines in 1865. Two years later, upon the death of his mother, he came under the influence of his wealthy guardian, Gustave Arosa, an antiquarian, photographer, and publisher, and a collector of modern French painting, especially Eugène Delacroix and the Barbizon School. By 1874, Gauguin—now married to the Danish Mette Gad and working as a stockbroker—was an amateur painter. He visited the first Impressionist exhibition held that year in the former, Paris studios of the photographer Felix Nadar, and met Camille Pissarro. By 1878, Gauguin was on his way to becoming a full-time artist. He exhibited with the Impressionists in 1880, and the following year attracted the attention of no less than the great novelist and critic Joris-Karl Huysmans, for his un-idealized, nude portrait of *Suzanne Sewing* (1880, p. 14).

In this early work, and in subsequent paintings such as *Young Woman at a Window–The Fiancé* (1888) Gauguin examined the particulars of women's labor, physiognomy and comportment with an ethnographer's care, and an indifference (surprising considering his later work in Tahiti), to their sexual being. His *Suzanne Sewing* depicts a mature woman with a decidedly plebian, naked body, engaged in the work of mending her clothes, perhaps her own underwear. The *Young Woman at a Window* represents a person about whom we know nothing, except that she is, as inscribed on the canvas, someone's *fiancé*. She has a flinty expression and mannish bearing, and wears a jacket and a type of *fez*, the brimless, conical, red hats worn by men in Turkey, Egypt and elsewhere in the Islamic world. The portrayal recalls Gauguin's fascination at this time and later, with androgyny, and the issue of women's rights. In a letter to Madeleine Bernard (sister of the artist Emile), from 1888, he counseled: "If...you want to be someone, to find happiness solely in your independence and your conscience...you must regard yourself as Androgyne, without sex....The virtues of a woman are exactly the same as the virtues of a man."[8] These attitudes, inherited in part from his maternal grandmother, Flora Tristan, would gradually evolve into a broader, golden age vision of the harmony and interdependence of the sexes. In Tahiti, Gauguin later wrote, "There is something virile in the women and feminine in the men.... [Here] man and woman are comrades, friends rather than lovers, dwelling almost without cease,

• • •

7 Flora Tristan, *Le Tour de France. Journal Inédite. 1843-44,* Paris, 1973, p. 86; cited in Georges Wildenstein, Sylvie Crussard and Martine Heudron, Catalogue Raisonné, Gauguin. A Savage in the Making. Paris and Milan: Skira, 2002, vol. 1, p. xxv.

8 Maurice Malingue (ed.), *Paul Gauguin: Letters to his Wife and Friends,* translated by Henry J. Stenning. Cleveland and New York: The World Publishing Company, 1949, p. 103.

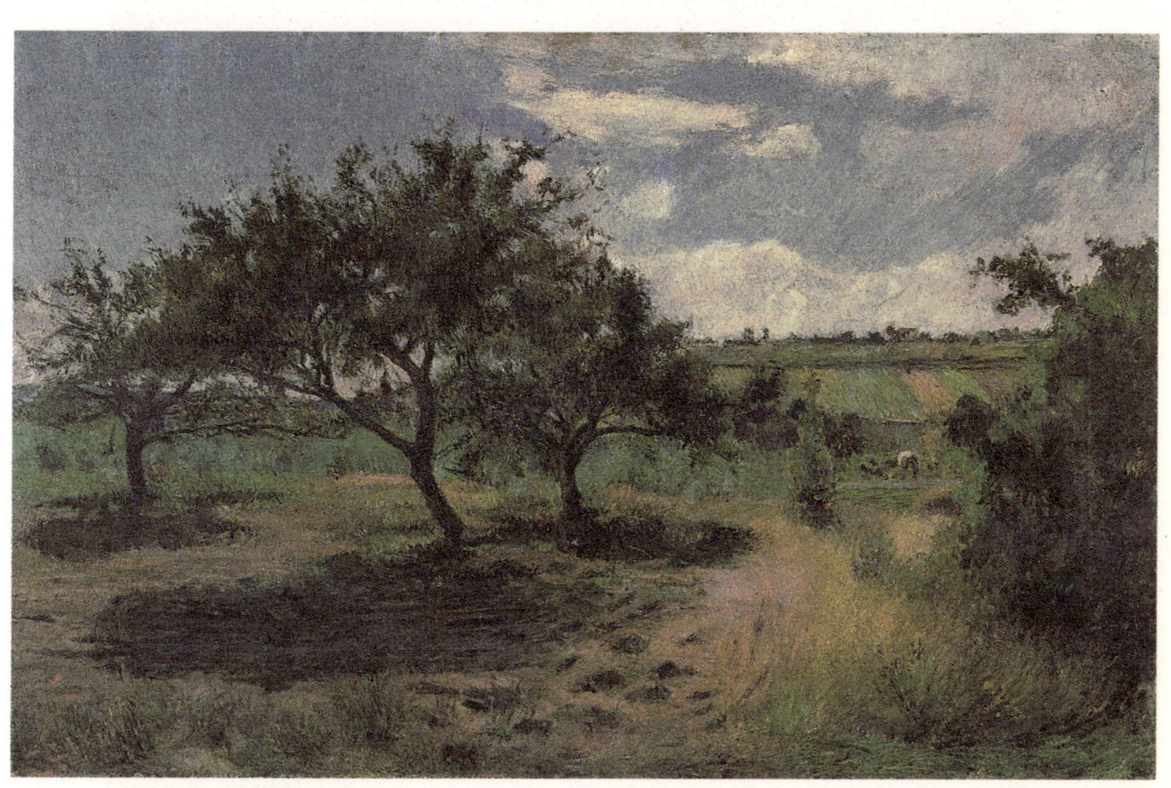

Apple Trees at L'Hermitage, Pontoise, 1879.
Oil on canvas, 65 × 100 cm.
Aargauer Kunsthaus, Aarau, Switzerland.

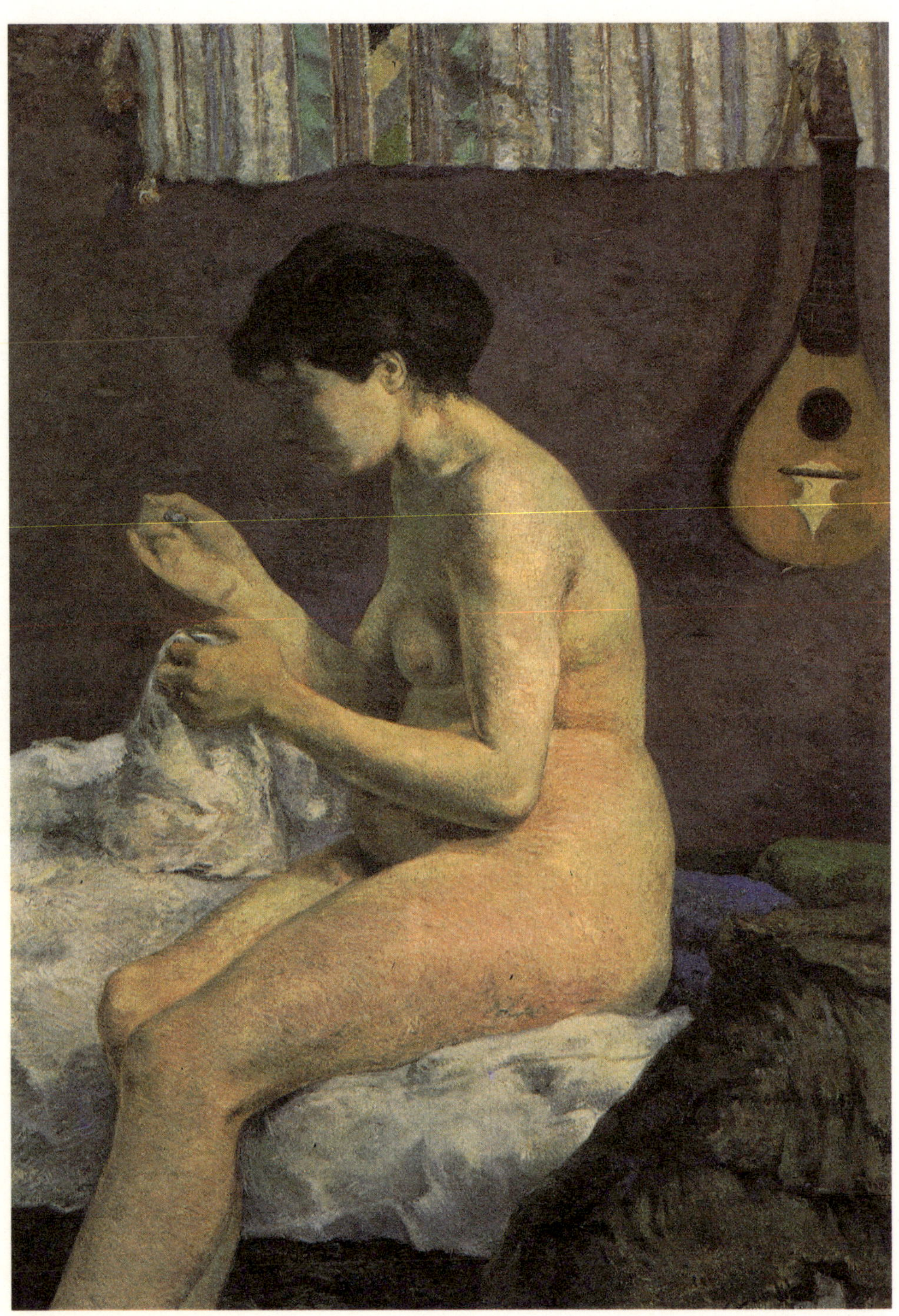

Study of a Nude or Susana Sewing, 1880.
Oil on canvas, 111.4 × 79.5 cm.
Ny Carlsberg Glyptotek,
Copenhagen.

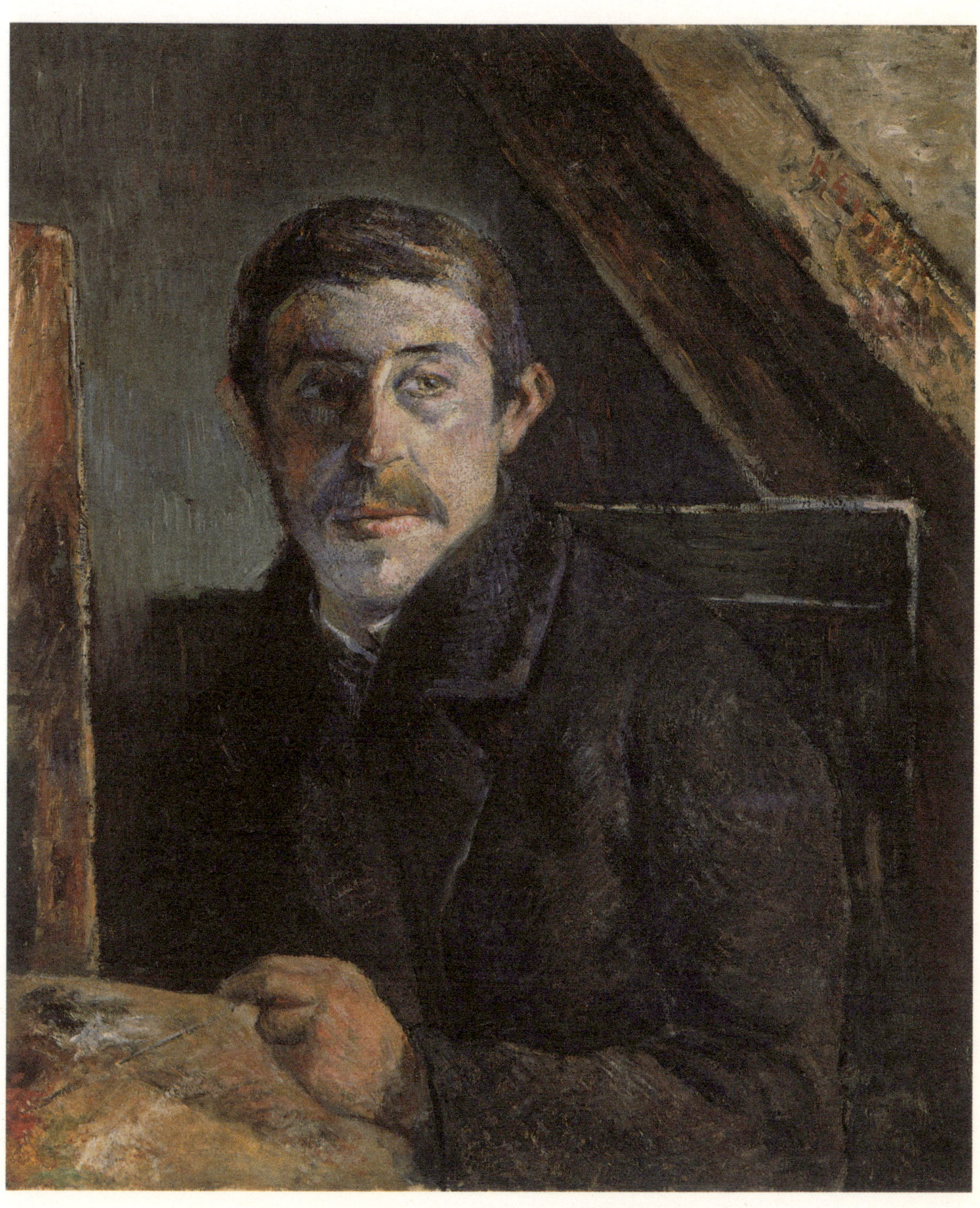

Self-Portrait, 1885.
Oil on canvas, 65 × 54 cm.
Private Collection, Bern.

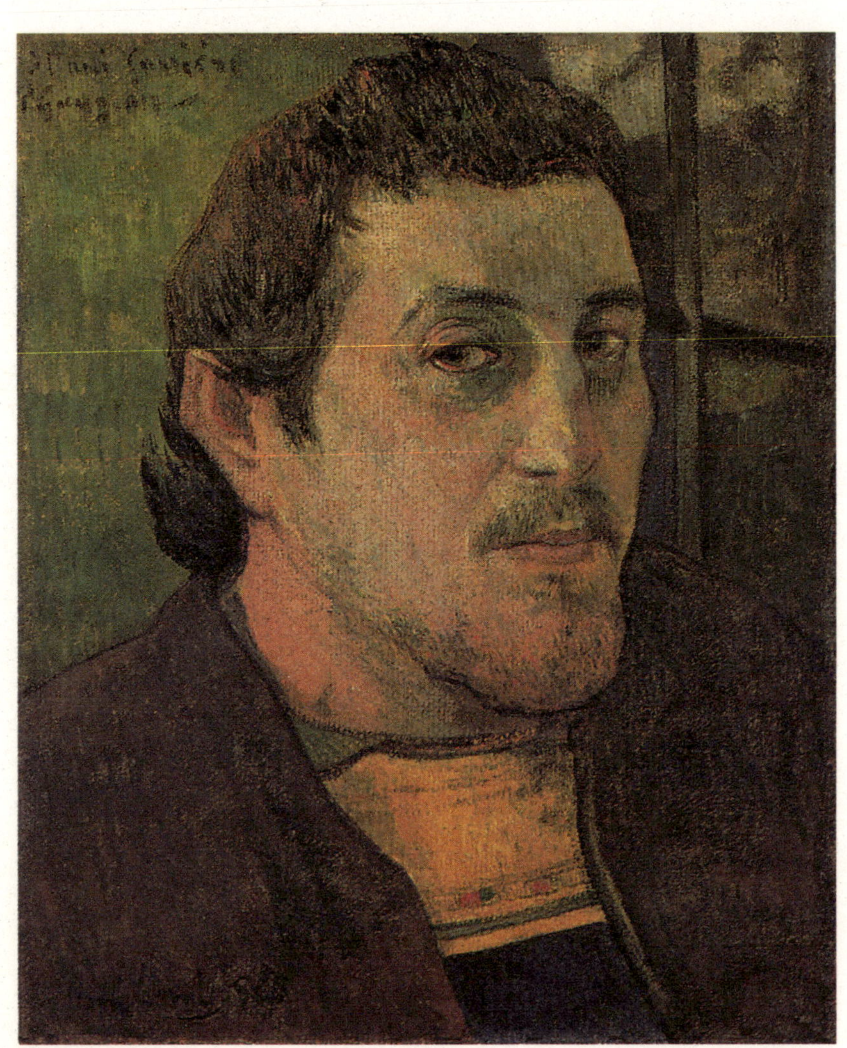

Self-Portrait Dedicated to Carrière, c. 1886.
Oil on canvas, 46.5 × 38.6 cm.
National Gallery of Art, Washington.

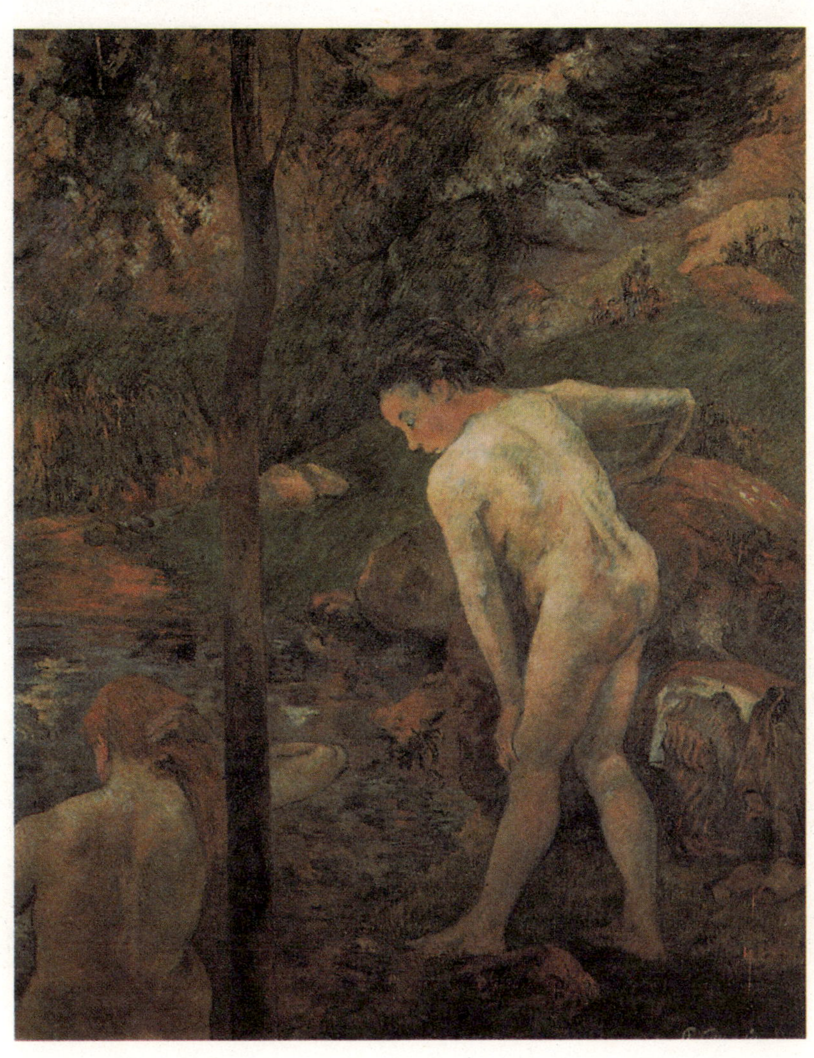

The Bather, 1887.
Oil on canvas, 87.5 × 70 cm.
Museo Nacional de Bellas
Artes, Buenos Aires.

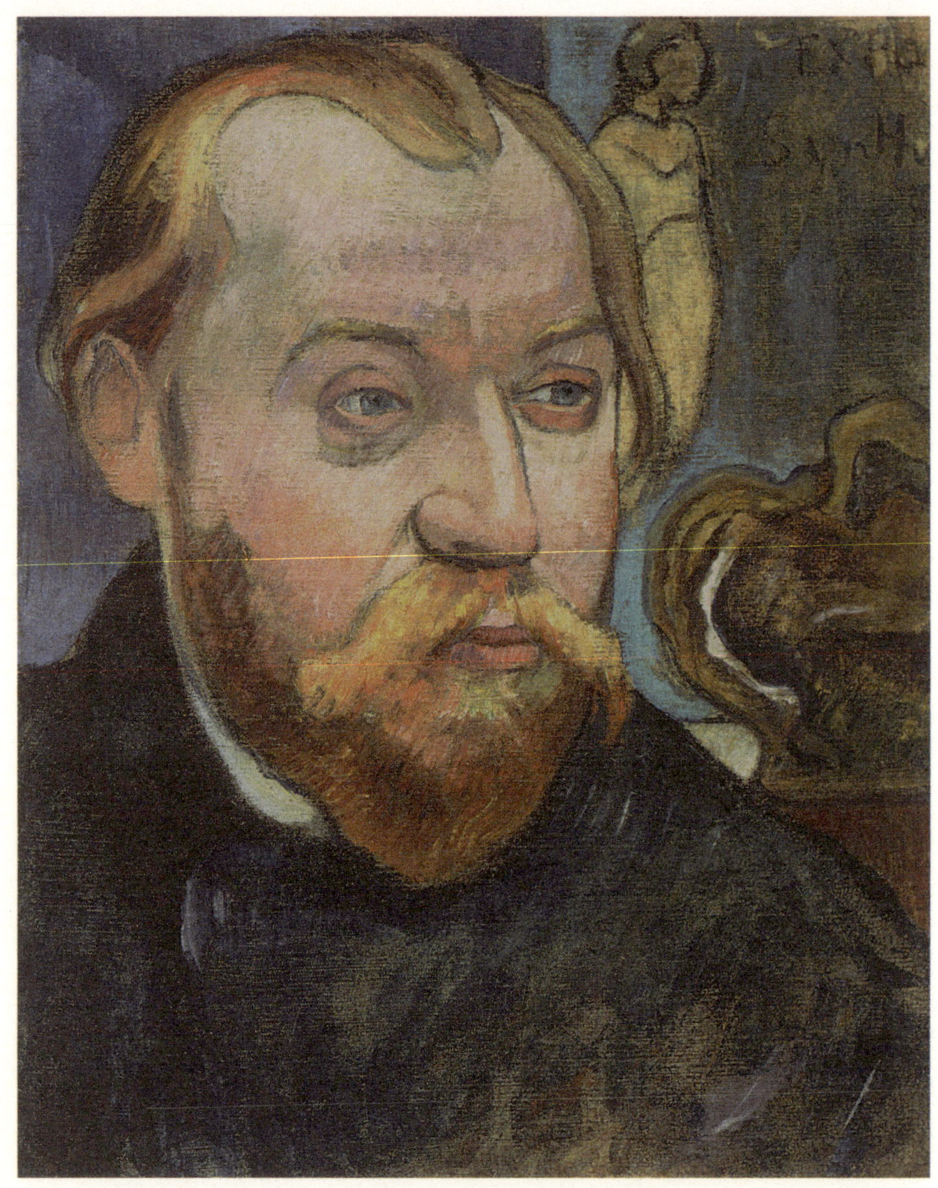

Portrait of Louis Roy, c 1883.
Oil on canvas, 40.5 × 32.5 cm.
Private Collection, New York.

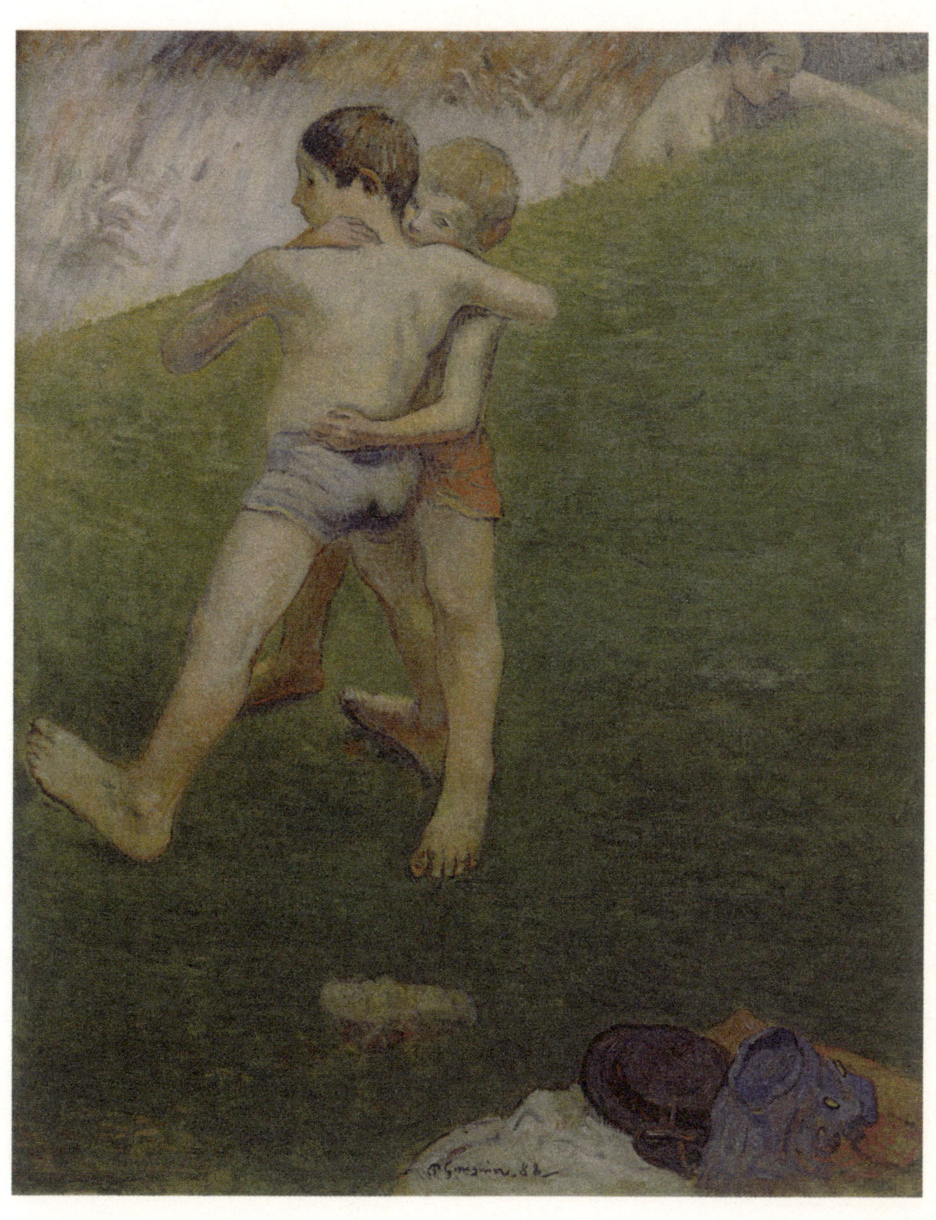

Young Wrestlers, 1888.
Oil on canvas, 93 × 73 cm.
Private Collection, Cleveland.

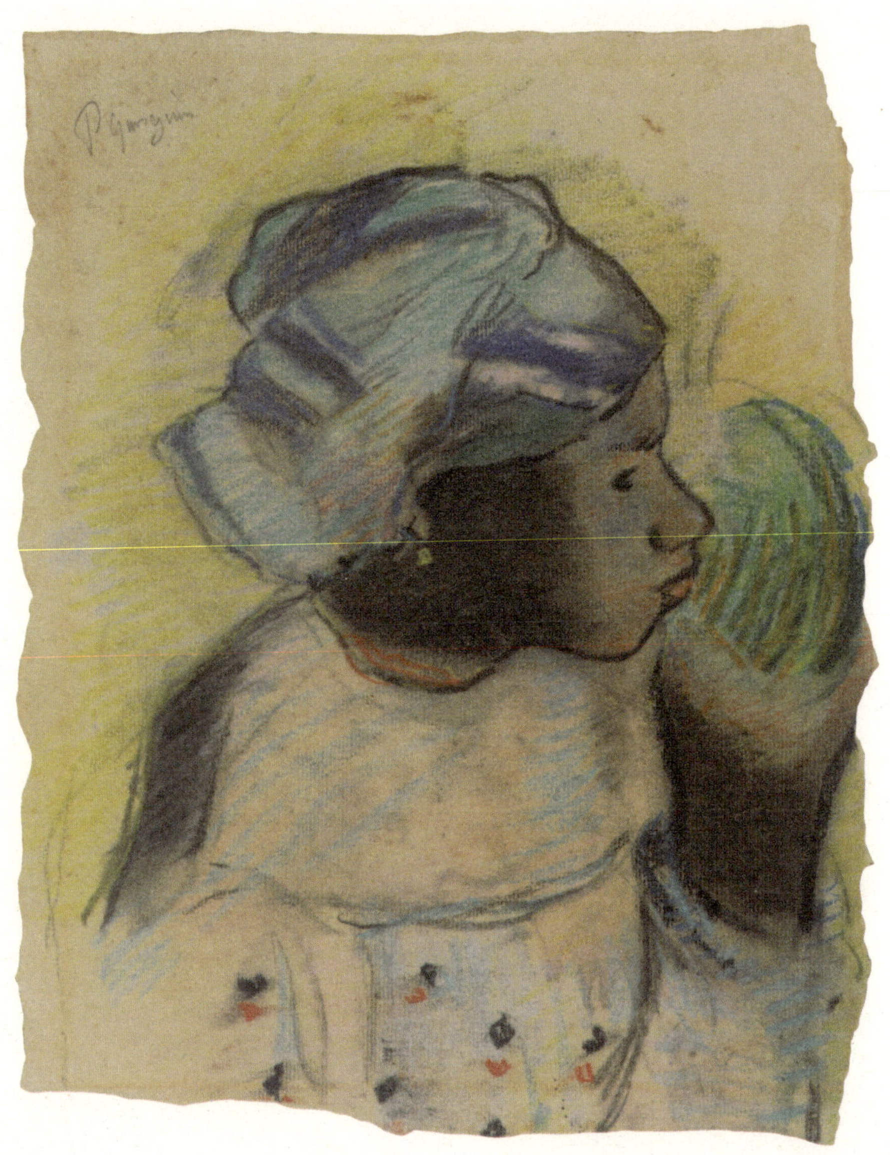

Head of a Woman, Martinique,
1887.
Chalk and pastel, 36 × 26 cm.
Van Gogh Museum, Amsterdam.

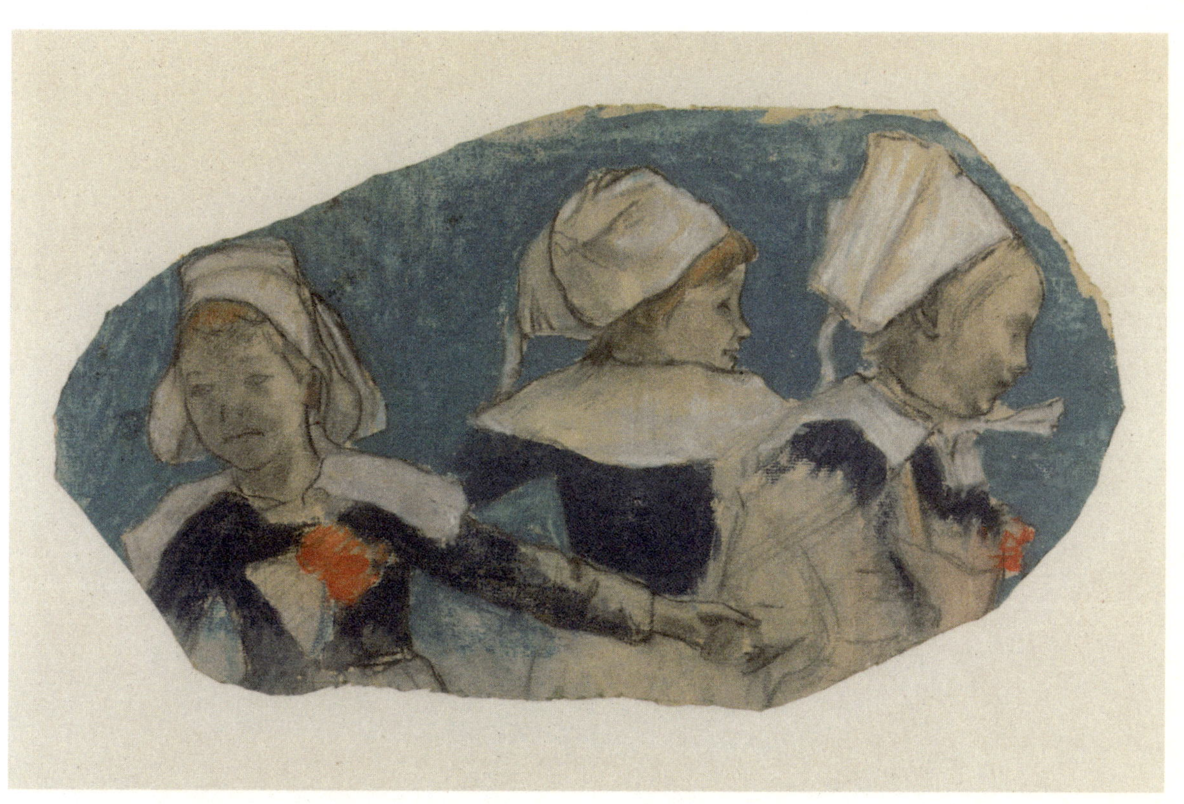

Study for "Breton Girls Dancing, Pont-Aven," 1888.
Brush and watercolor over charcoal and pastel,
24 × 41 cm.
Van Gogh Museum, Amsterdam.

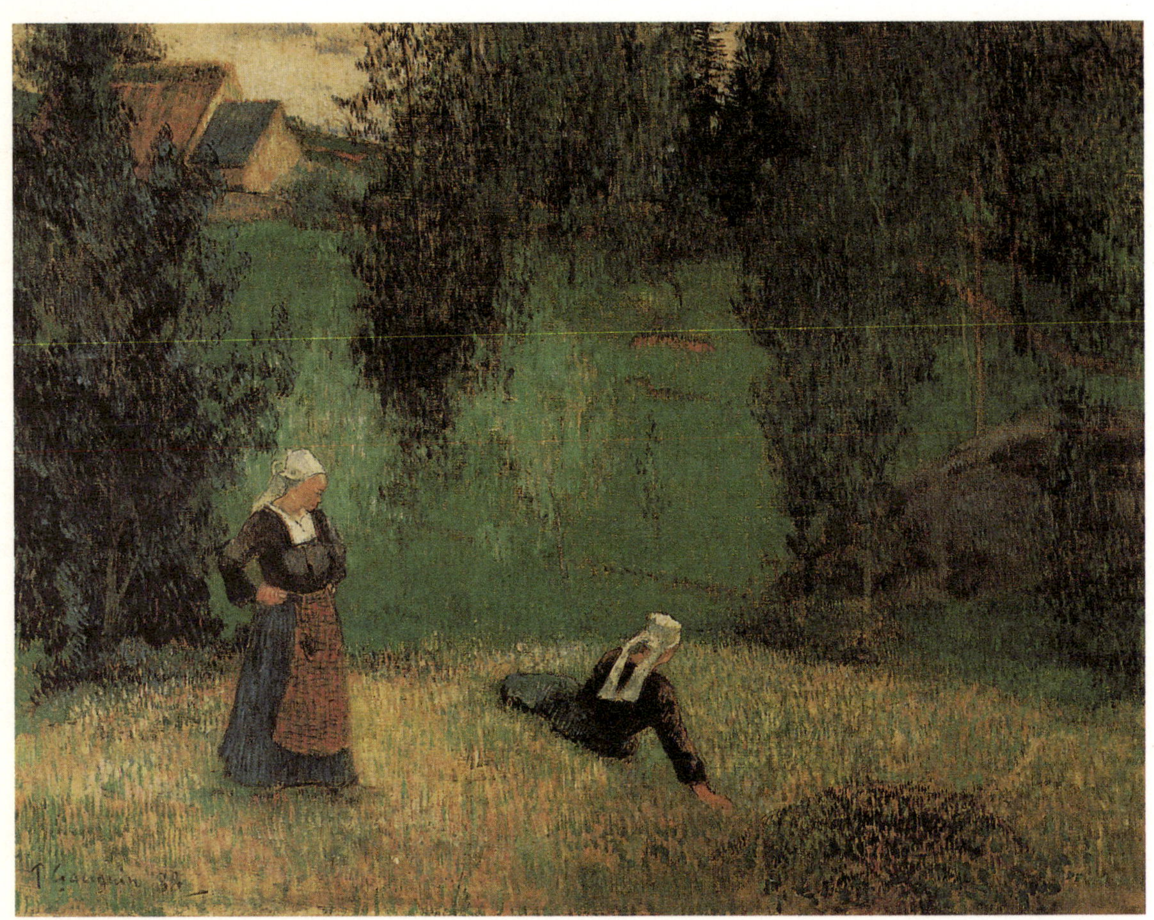

Early Flowers, 1888.
Oil on canvas, 73 × 92 cm.
On loan to the Kunsthaus, Zurich.

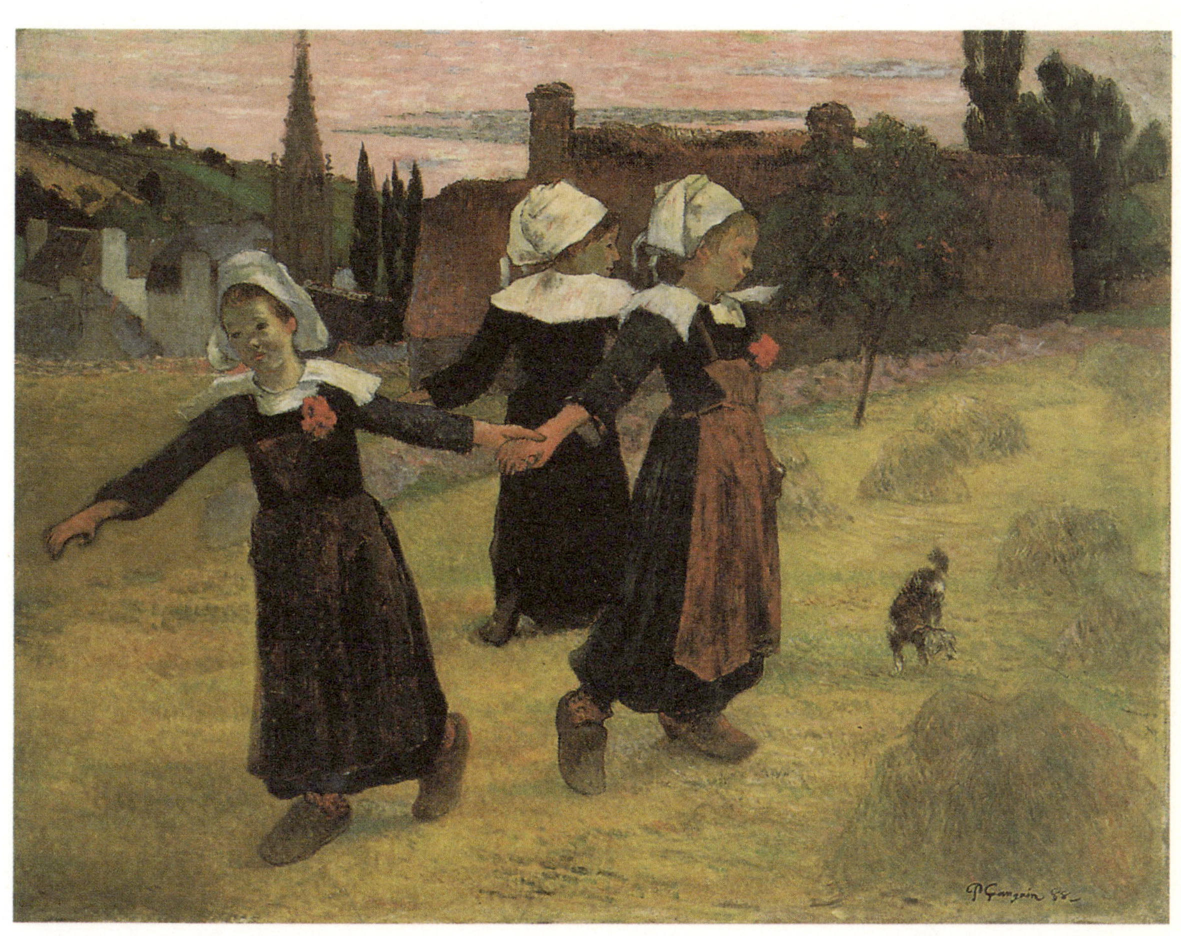

Breton Girls Dancing,
Pont-Aven, 1888.
Oil on canvas, 71.4 × 92.8 cm.
National Gallery of Art,
Washington.

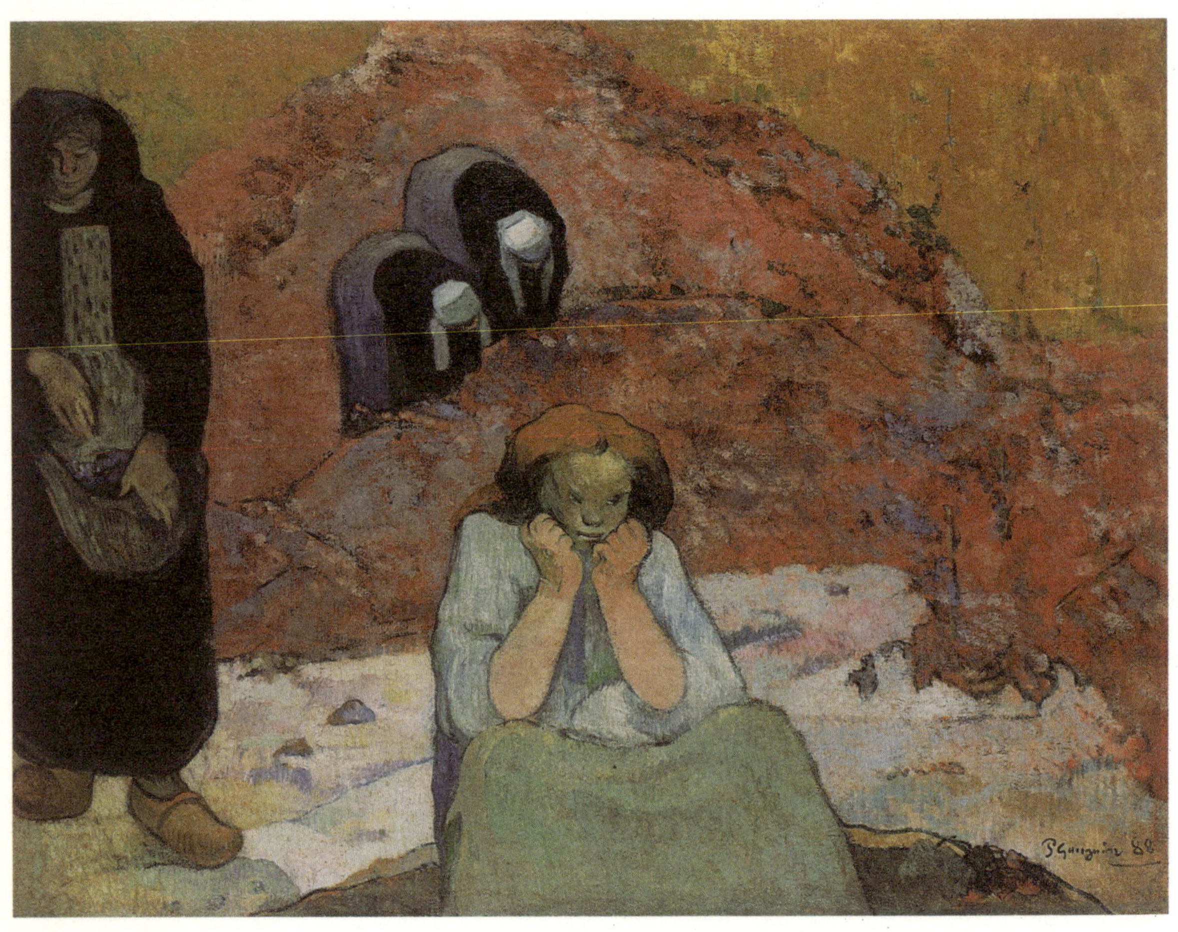

Human Misery, 1888.
Oil on canvas, 72.5 × 92 cm.
Ordrupgaard Museum,
Copenhagen.

in pain and in pleasure, and even the very idea of vice is unknown to them."[9] That attitude would be exemplified by, among other works, *Vahine no te tiare* (*Woman with Flowers,* 1891-92), a figure of grandeur and calm who recalls nothing so much us *Mona Lisa,* and *Nave nave moe*, with its figures dreaming, eating, dancing or bathing in a sacred spring. But before the artist could travel to this idealized, utopian terrain, he would have to navigate the difficult, local waters of bourgeois commerce and artistic competition.

The Dream Visions of Brittany, Martinique and Arles. In 1882, Gauguin's fortunes fell. A stock market crash led to a broad economic down-turn, and by autumn of the following year, he had quit the brokerage business. However he had already determined his future the year before, as revealed by a letter written to his friend, the Impressionist painter Camille Pissarro:

> Business is at a very low ebb, and the future isn't looking too great....My mind is completely taken up with dreams, observing nature and the desire to work, and little by little I just forget about business or at least how to do business. As for giving up painting even for a minute, Never!

In fact, there would be one more business interregnum before he settled permanently into the life of an artist, and that came near the end of 1884, when Gauguin, in order to save money, moved with his Danish wife and their children to Copenhagen. There he took a job as a tarpaulin salesman, while continuing to make art in his spare time. His *Self-Potrait* (1885) from this time, reveals clearly enough the narrowed circumstances of his new life. Pressed beneath a dormer or steeply sloped ceiling, the artist, pulled close to the surface of real and fictive paintings, sits on a high-backed, wooden chair, gazing expressionless into a mirror as he tips his brush into some red paint. It must be a cold spring day, because he is wearing a heavy jacket, and the family only moved to the house with the attic studio on Norregade street on April 22. Unable to speak Danish, and without the stimulation of friends and allies, Gauguin felt himself cut off from the world of art. "I am more tormented by art than ever and I'm not distracted from it by either money torments or business inquiries...I console myself by dreaming."[10] Now, as Gauguin's daily responsibilities and routines closed in upon him, his dreams of a Virgilian Golden Age became even more fervid, linked to the achievement of Paul Cézanne, whom he had admired and come to know since 1881, and whose works he had even begun to collect. In a letter to Schuffenecker from January 1885, he wrote about the artist from Provence:

> A man of the south, he spends whole days reading Virgil and contemplating the sky. Therefore his goals are lofty, his blues of great intensity and the red in his work has an astonishing reverberation. Like [the work of] Virgil, which has many senses and can be interpreted at will, the literature of his paintings has a parabolic sense with two purposes; his backgrounds are as imaginative as they are real."[11]

The description anticipates the arc of Gauguin's own works made a few years later, derived from fantasy and reality, dreams and materiality. It also reveals the artist's subtle understanding of the ancient Roman author, who blended the hard facts of agriculture with the freedom of fantasy, and who even drew distinctions (especially in *The Aeneid*), between true and false dreams: those

• • •

9 Paul Gauguin, *Noa Noa*, translated by O.F. Theis. New York: Dover Publ., 1985, p. 20.

10 *Correspondence*, edited by Victor Merlhés, p. 65.

11 *Correspondence*, edited by Victor Merlhés, p. 65.

that foretell, and those that falsely represent the future.[12] But as yet Gauguin had few opportunities to try his own variations on these Virgilian principles. These months were among the least productive of his life, and by June 1885 he was back in Paris, with his son Clovis, his wife left behind in Denmark.

In Paris, Gauguin's thoughts turned constantly to his art, the dream of independence, and the models of Pissarro and Cézanne. Sometime in 1886, he painted a very Cézanne-like *Portrait of Clovis*, his 7 year-old son, unsmiling, gazing intensely at the viewer, and holding in his lap a book as big as his torso. The painting resembles Cézanne's portrait of his own son, painted before Gauguin's picture, and is marked by a surprising pictorial abstraction and emotional flatness. It was at this time too, in early 1886, that Gauguin began to make ceramics, partly under the inspiration and tutelage of Ernest Chaplet, who had been trained at the Sèvres factory, and who pioneered the French revival of stoneware. Gauguin's own work in the medium was extremely varied, from the elegant, Japanese-inspired colored slipware of *Vase Decorated with Breton Scenes*,(1886-7) to the strange, animated, brutal and purposely misshapen *Vase with Half-Length Figure* (1886-7). Gauguin was particularly attracted to forms derived from Peruvian (Moche) pottery. These ancient ceramics were made between 100 and 800 AE, and often took the form of human heads, or featured blatantly sexual subjects and forms. Many of Gauguin's ceramics, including the *Pot in the Shape of a Martiniquan Woman's Head* and *Pot with Breton Figure* (both, 1887) conform to this Andean model. The former consists of a single, unglazed, but partially painted head, and the second is a double-vase with stirrup handle and wide, sheath-like or vaginal opening. Gauguin would continue to work in this medium whenever he was in Paris and had access to clay and kiln.

Seeking an inexpensive place to live as well as the company of fellow artists, Gauguin traveled to Pont–Aven, in Brittany, in the summer of 1886, continuing the Impressionist experiments begun in Dieppe, but now with a still greater freedom and confidence. The *Still Life with Portrait of Laval* (1886) provides a pretty good summary of the artist's achievements to date. It is at once Cézannesque and utterly original; the haphazard piling of fruits on a white cloth, and emphasis upon modulation of hue, is an unmistakable sign of the influence of the master from Aix, but the flatness of form and uniformity of color establishes a different direction in the history of art. Neither still life nor portrait, the painting is in fact an homage to Gauguin himself, since it represents his friend, the painter Charles Laval's rapt attention to a particularly bizarre (and now lost) ceramic by Gauguin. The painting is also significant because it reveals the rudiments of a new style of painting—partly inspired by Pissarro and Cézanne but conceived in collaboration with Émile Bernard, which sympathetic critics would soon label "cloisonnism," because of its use of clear, dark contour lines recalling the technique of medieval, cloisonné enamel. The hard outlines around the fruit, the ceramic, and Laval's profile, hint at the pictorial flatness and abstraction that would fully emerge a year or so later with *Vision After the Sermon (Jacob Wrestling with the Angel,* 1888, p. 27), a painting that was singled out for special praise in 1891 by the young critic Albert Aurier. In his article "Symbolism in Painting: Paul Gauguin," Aurier heralded the arrival of a new art that paralleled the idealist school of poetry associated with Paul Verlaine, Arthur Rimbaud, and Stéphane Mallarmé. The non-naturalist colors and outlines, and the dream-like character of the scene (the Breton women in the foreground imagine the biblical drama visible at right), combine to convey an abstraction far removed from Impressionist norms. In fact, Gauguin had already, the previous year employed vivid, and non-naturalist colors, and a highly contrived, decorative touch

• • •

12 Nicholas Reed, "The Gates of Sleep in *Aeneid 6*", *The Classical Quarterly*, vol. 23, no. 2, 1973, pp. 311-315.

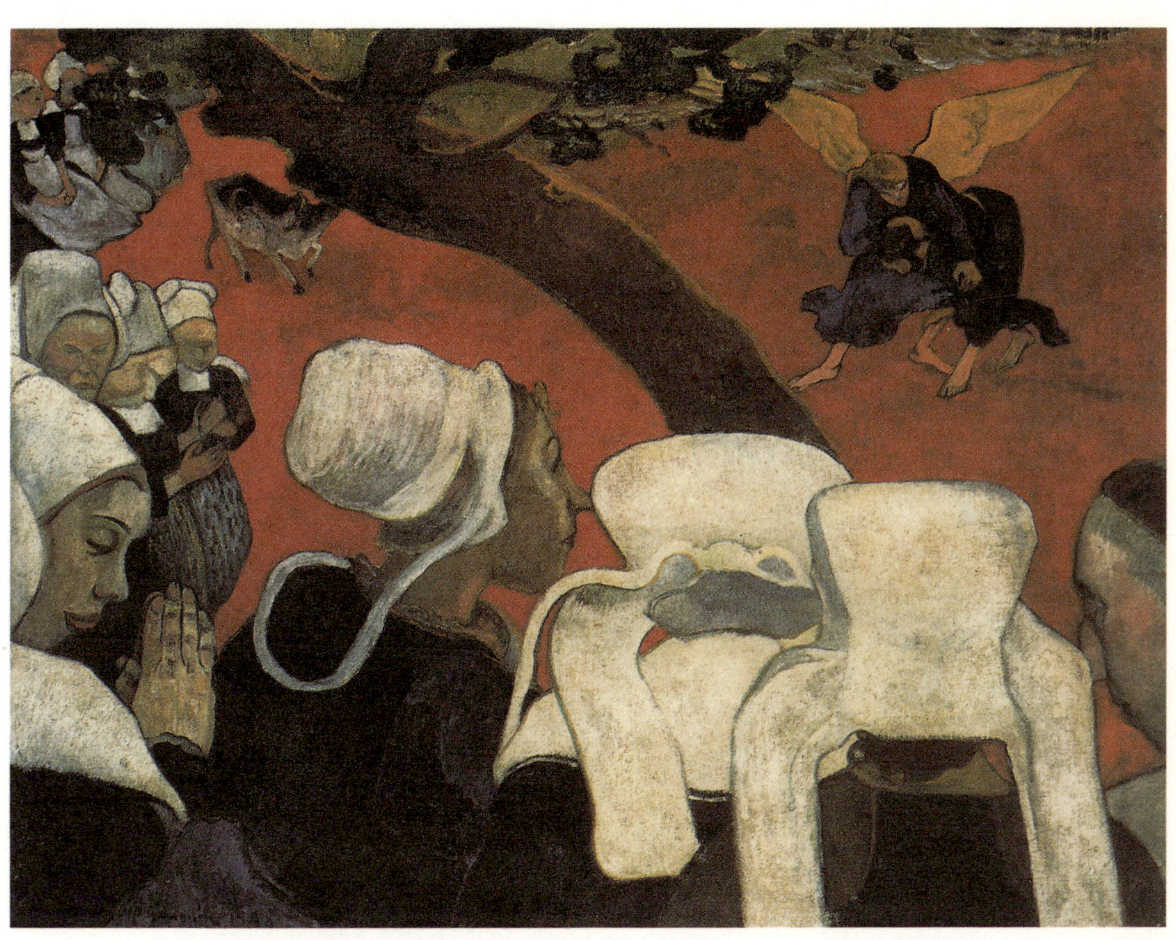

Vision after the Sermon (Jacob Wrestling with the Angel), 1888. Oil on canvas, 72.1 × 91 cm. National Gallery of Scotland, Edinburgh.

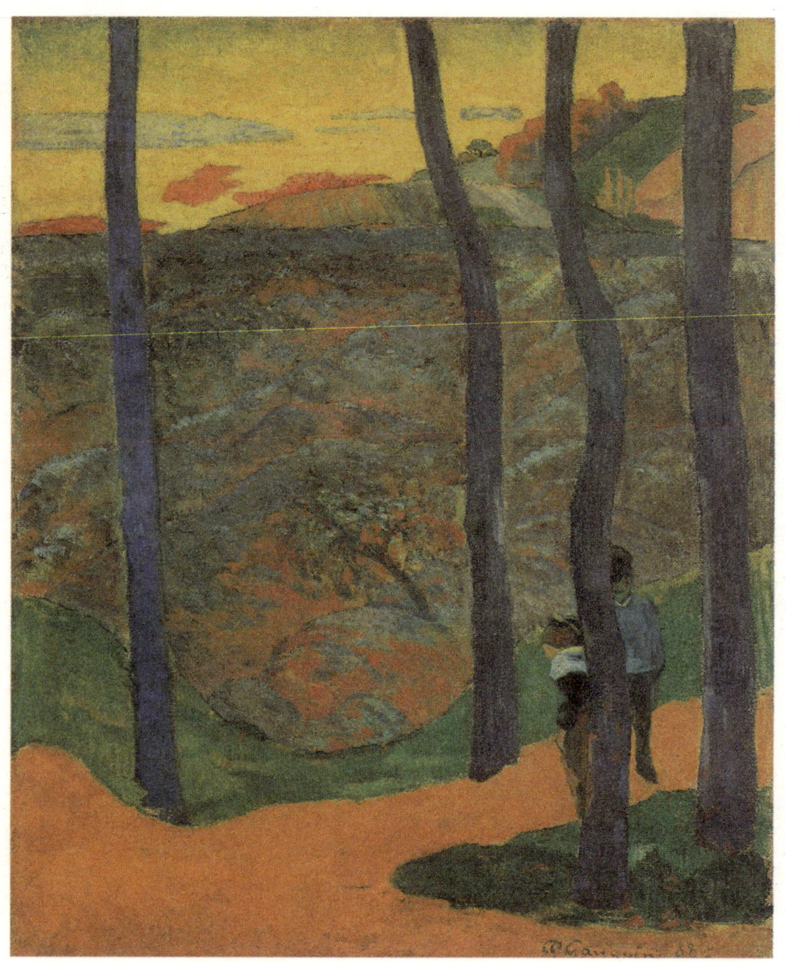

The Blue Tree Trunks, 1888.
Oil on canvas, 92 × 73 cm.
Ordrupgaard Museum,
Copenhagen.

during his trip—in the company of Laval—to the island of Martinique in the Carribbean. In certain works from that brief period, including *Saint-Pierre Roadstead*, the color is very bright, and the composition highly abstract, betokening the fecundity of a magical land, as Virgil had written of his paradise, where "the ground will not suffer the mattock, nor the vine the pruning hook," and "native scarlet shall clothe the lambs at their pasturage." Saint-Pierre Roadstead is also an invocation of Japan, regularly invoked by Gauguin and later Van Gogh as a veritable utopia where artists lived freely, communally and without competition. The landscape closely resembles Hokusai's *Hodogaya on the Tokaido Road* from the *"Thirty-six Views of Mount Fuji."* Each is comprised of a foreground with a screen of trees, and a few figures and animals, framing a distant volcano. Indeed, the resemblance is so strong, that the print must be considered a direct source for the painting, just as Hokusai's Mangwa and Hiroshige's Blossoming Plum Trees were sources for *Vision of the Sermon* a year later.

During Gauguin's short but turbulent stay with Vincent van Gogh (1853–1890) in Arles in late 1888 (ending with the self-mutilation of the younger Dutch painter), he continued his experiments with outline, abstraction and seemingly arbitrary color choice. His *Night Cafe* (1888) features the alert and wary proprietress of the establishment, Mme. Ginoux seated in the extreme foreground beside a table with a tall glass for absinthe, a siphon and a plate with two sugar cubes. Behind her are a billiard table (with cat perched against its nearest leg), and six denizens of this working-class bar. The colors are divided into neat, rectangular blocks—white, brown, green, ochre, orange—and each is separated from the other by dark lines, like wires. Here, in Van Gogh's world, there is for Gauguin little space for utopia, no glimpse of a past or future Golden Age. After the Christmas Eve debacle, Gauguin beat a hasty retreat to the north.

In early 1889, Gauguin returned to Brittany. There he resumed his search for what he called the savage and the primitive, that is, for a place that might offer him refuge from European property relations. In letters and diaries, he lamented the oppression of what he called in a letter to the painter Willumsen in 1889, the "kingdom of gold," and expressed his desire to live in a place where direct exchange or even a gift economy prevailed, where "material life can be lived without money."[13] Brittany must at first have seemed to Gauguin to be such a place. The close-knit character of the communities of Western Brittany, where an ancient Celtic language was still spoken and where traditional costumes were worn on special holidays and religious festivals, were signs of human values trumping economic ones. Moreover, the land itself must have seemed at first glance to be free and open to all; during the *pardons*, men, women and children walked and danced across open fields, meadows and orchards, unrestrained by walls, fences or other marks of property division. This transgression of boundaries is depicted in the background of *The Yellow Christ* (1889, p. 40). But Gauguin must also have reflected upon his own evident exclusion from this pre-capitalist, Arcadian free space. He lived in hotels and inns, not in homes and farms; he bought meals in taverns and restaurants, rather than cooking them himself from plants and animals he had grown and raised; and he could not in good conscience join in the religious or secular processions that constituted the core of Breton symbolic life. This rich and affective Breton world was closed to the modern, metropolitan artist, and Gauguin reflected upon that fact in "Breton Women at a Gate" from the *Volpini Suite* and other works concerned with barriers and obstacles. In *Bonjour M. Gauguin*, the artist depicts himself as a pilgrim, an exile, or "The Wandering Jew," as in Gustave Courbet's well-know canvas (inspired by folk legends and popular prints), *The Meeting*, aka *Bonjour M. Courbet* (1854). In Gauguin's picture, the artist is separated from a local Breton woman by a closed gate. He has lowered his cap by way of greeting, but received

• • •

13 "Une lettre inédite de Gauguin," *Les Marges*, vol. 14, May 1918, pp. 168-169.

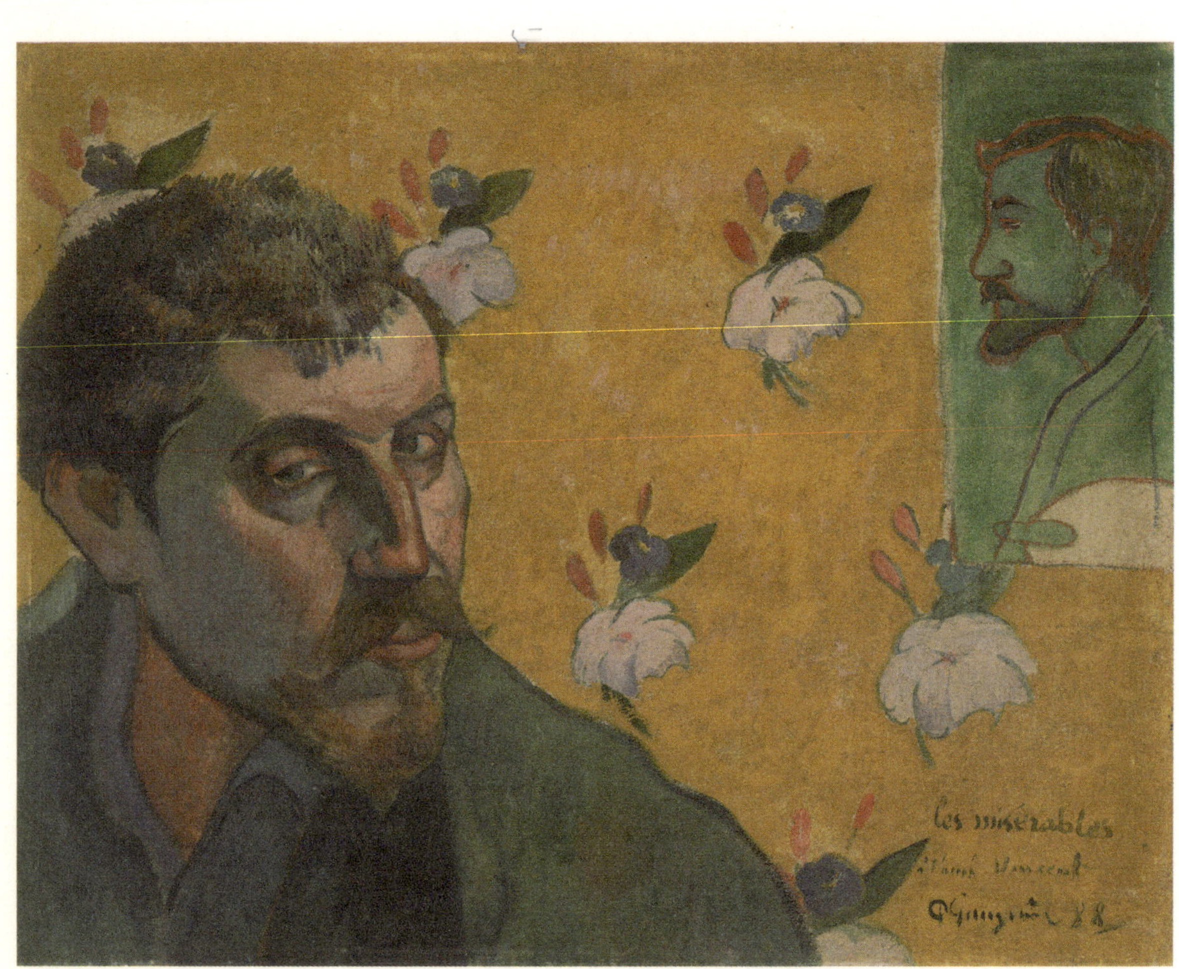

Self-Portrait (Les Misérables), 1888.
Oil on canvas, 45 × 55 cm.
Van Gogh Museum, Amsterdam.

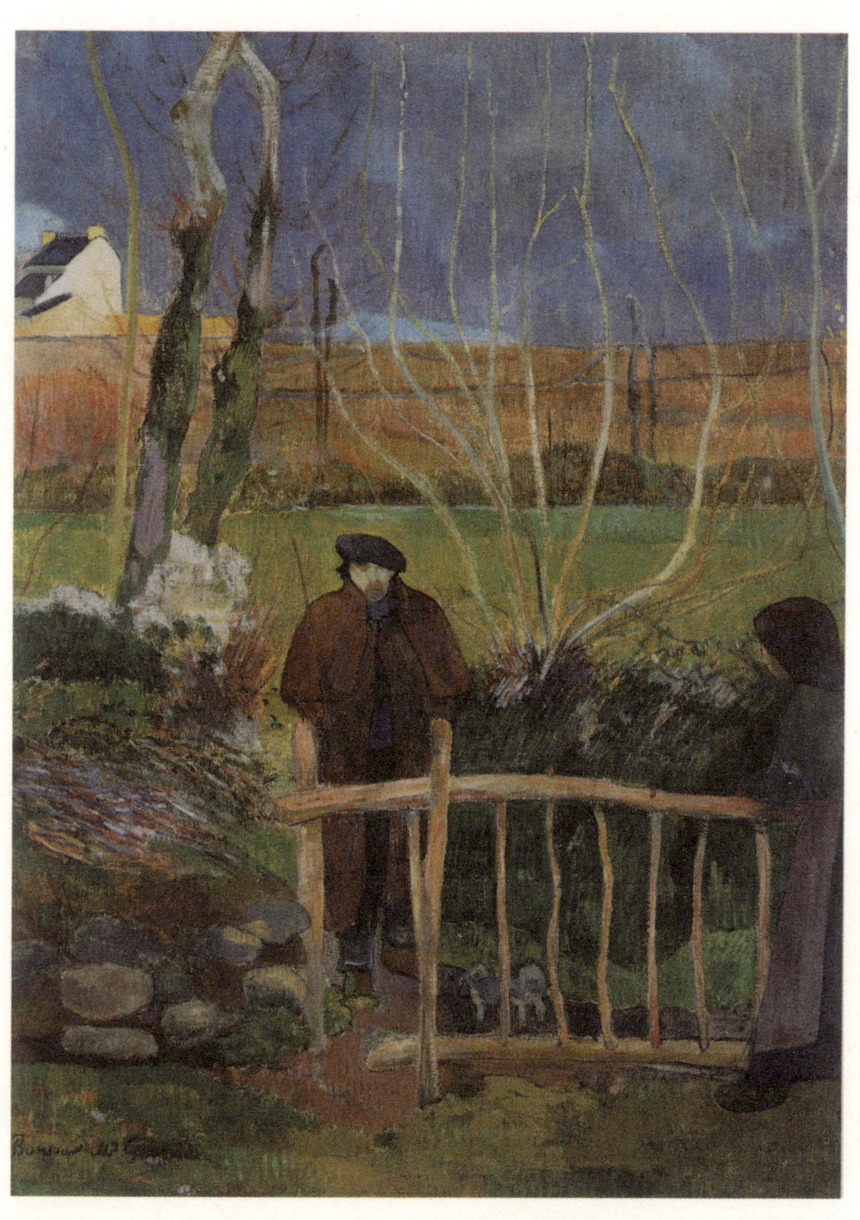

Bonjour Monsieur Gauguin,
1889.
Oil on canvas laid down on wood, 74.9 × 54.8 cm.
Hammer Museum, Los Angeles.

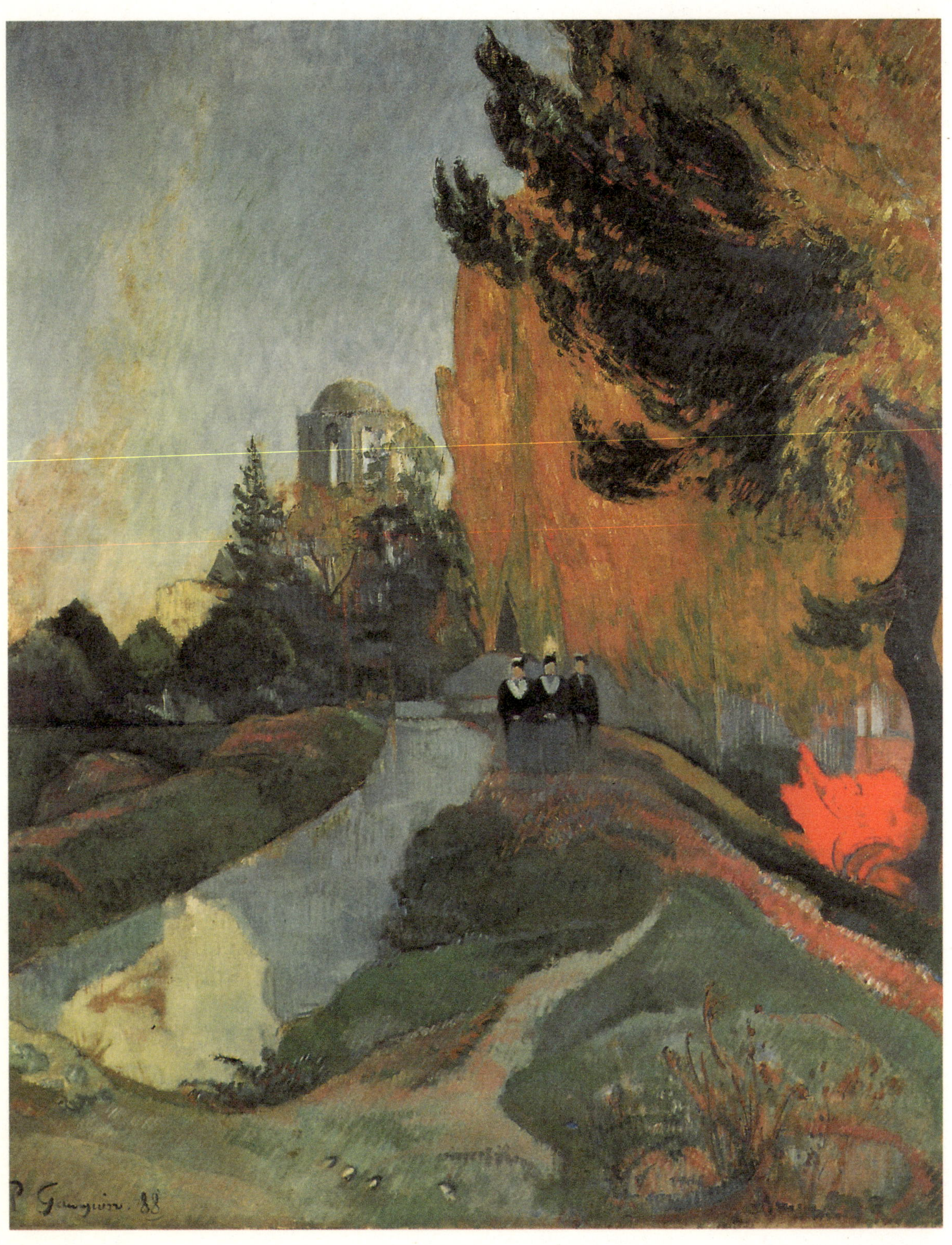

Les Alyscamps, 1888.
Oil on canvas, 92 × 73 cm.
Musée d'Orsay, Paris.

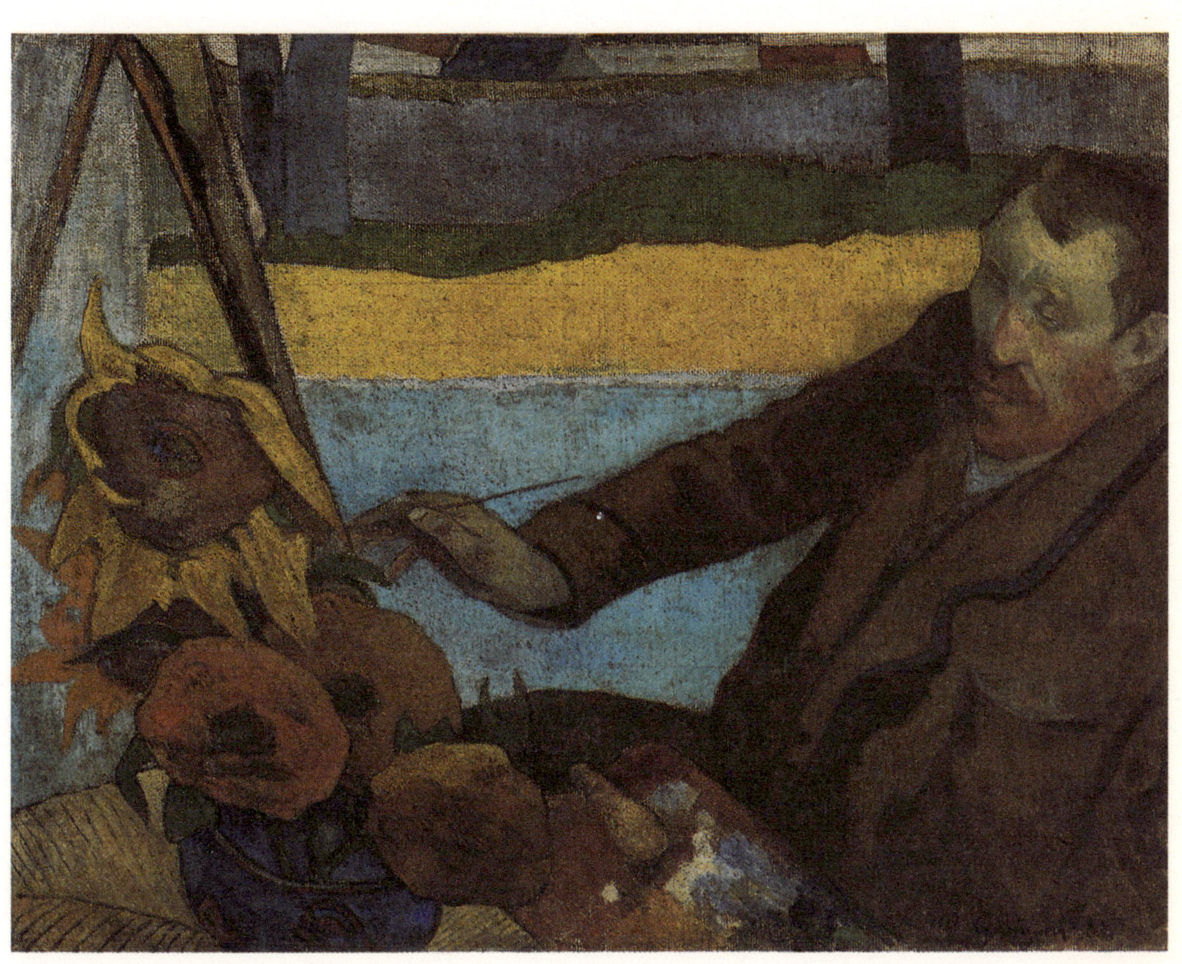

Van Gogh Painting Sunflowers,
1888.
Oil on canvas, 73 × 92 cm.
Rijksmuseum Vincent van Gogh,
Amsterdam.

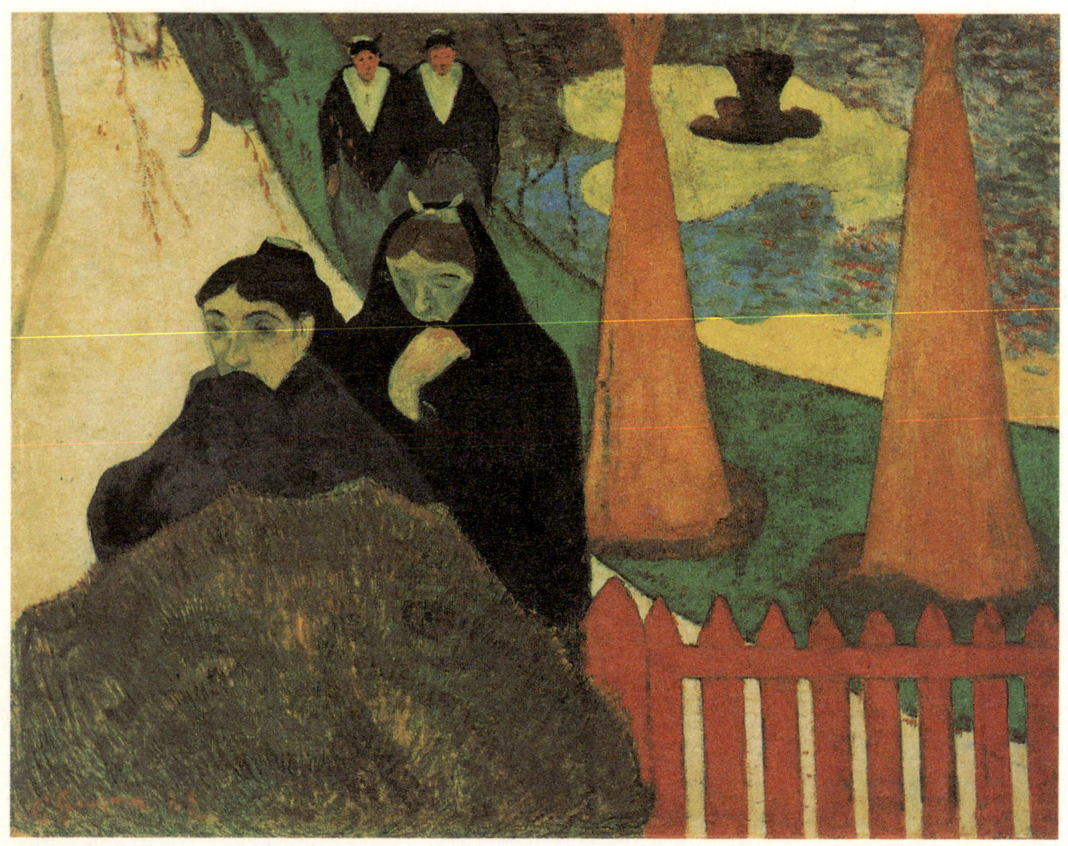

Old Women at Arles, 1888.
Oil on canvas, 73 × 92 cm.
The Art Institute of Chicago,
Chicago.

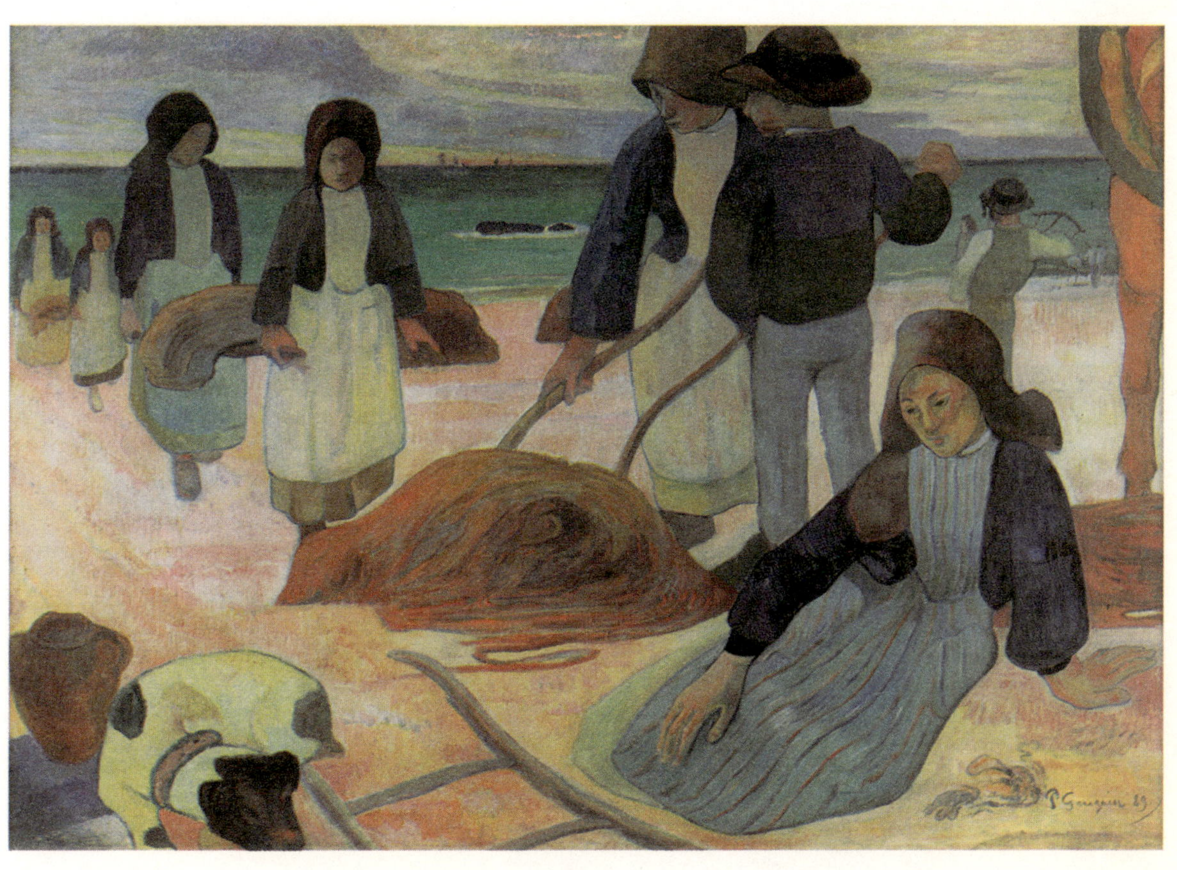

The Seaweed Gatherers, 1889.
Oil on canvas, 87 × 123 cm.
Museum Folkwang, Essen.

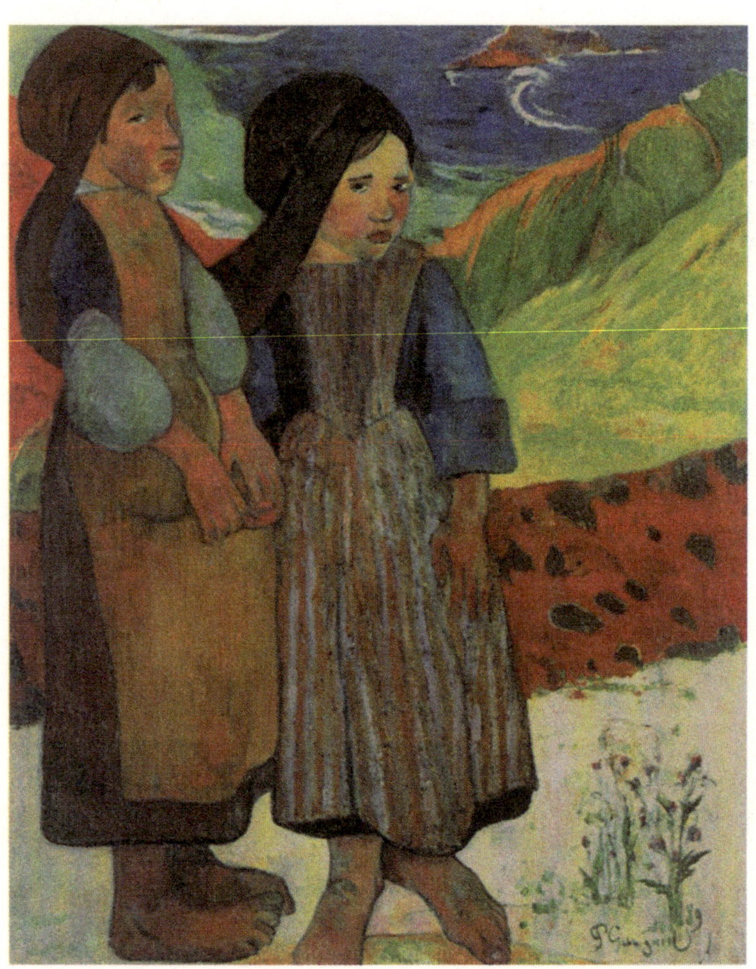

Two Breton Girls by the Sea,
1889.
Oil on canvas, 92 × 73 cm.
National Museum of Western
Art, Tokyo.

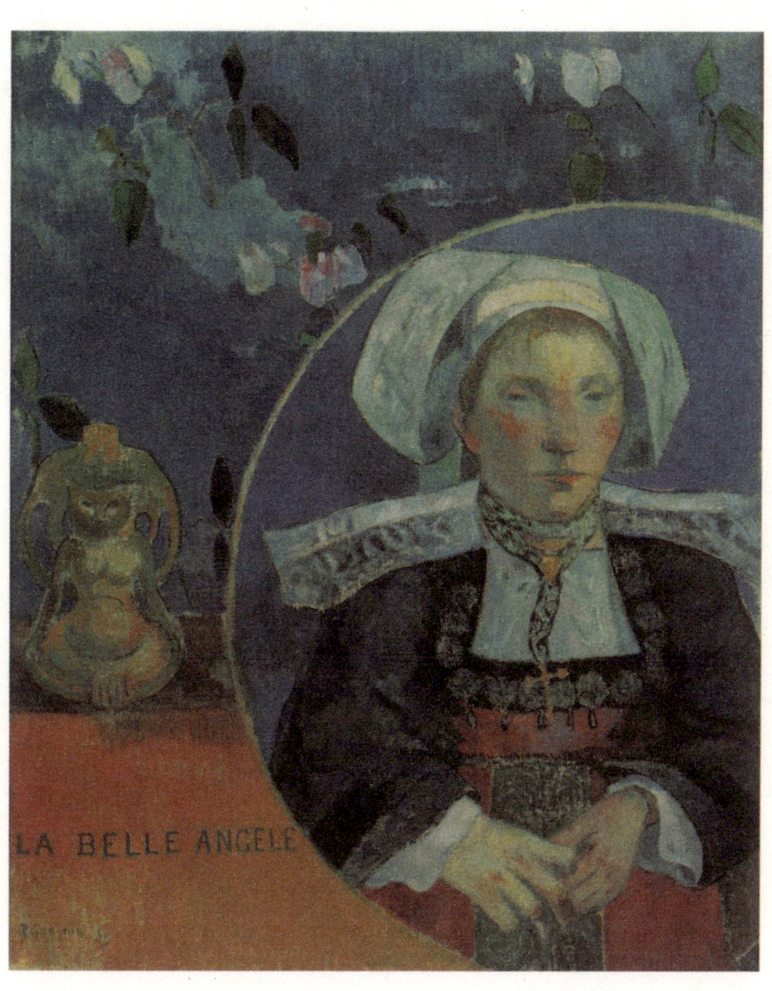

The Beautiful Angela, 1889.
Oil on canvas, 92 × 73 cm.
Musée d'Orsay, Paris.

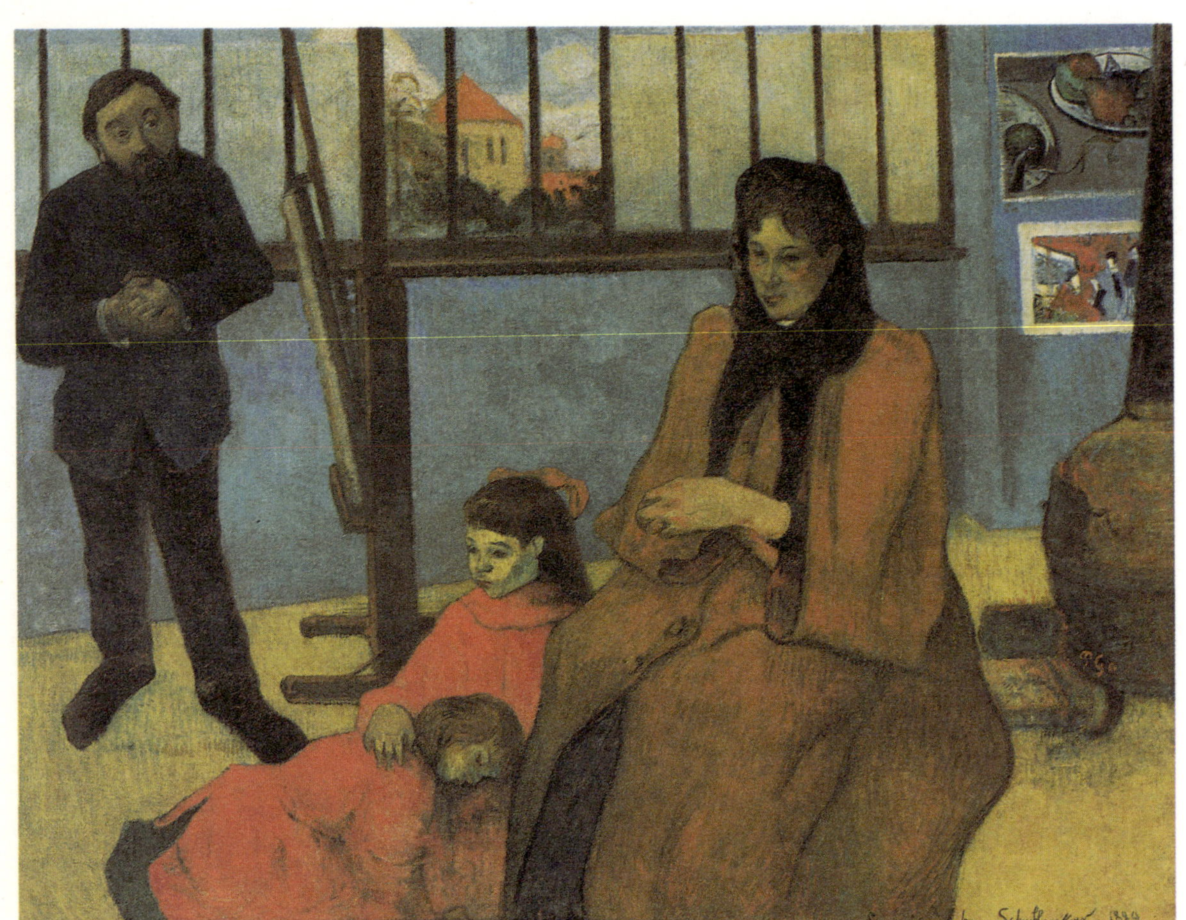

The Schuffenecker Family,
1889.
Oil on canvas, 73 × 92 cm.
Musée d'Orsay, Paris.

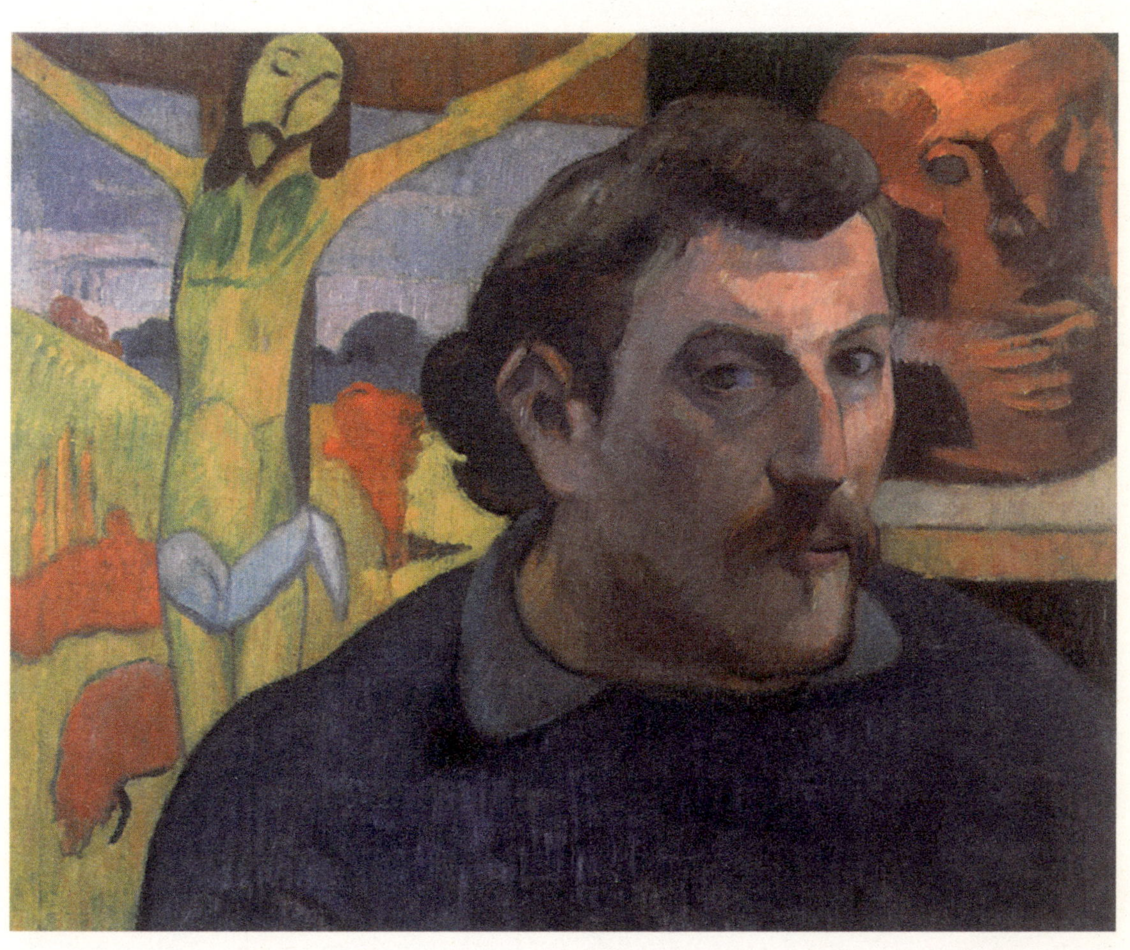

Self-Portrait with Yellow Christ, 1889–1890.
Oil on canvas, 38 × 46 cm.
Private Collection.

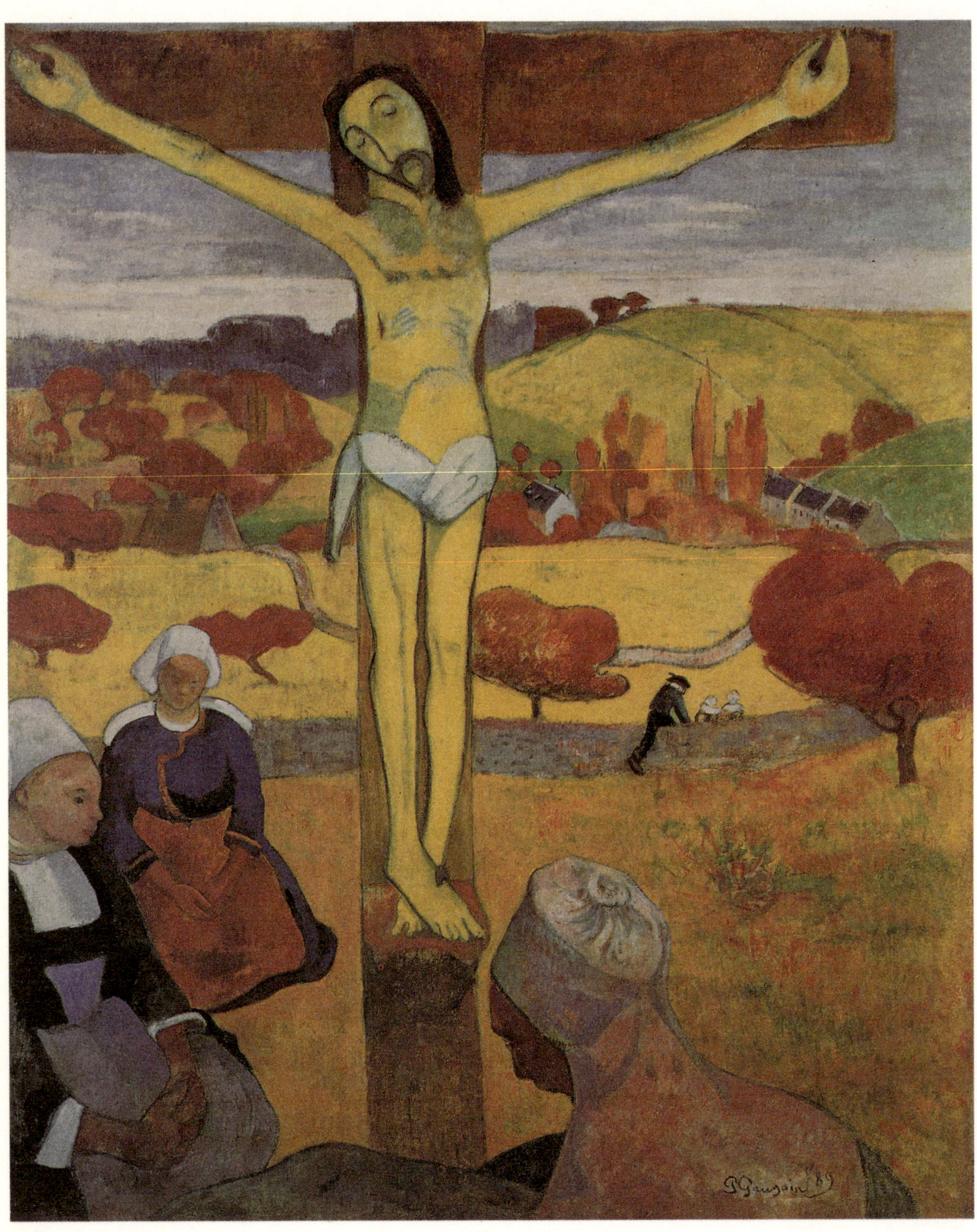

The Yellow Christ, 1889.
Oil on canvas, 93 × 73 cm.
Albright-Knox Art Gallery,
Buffalo, New York.

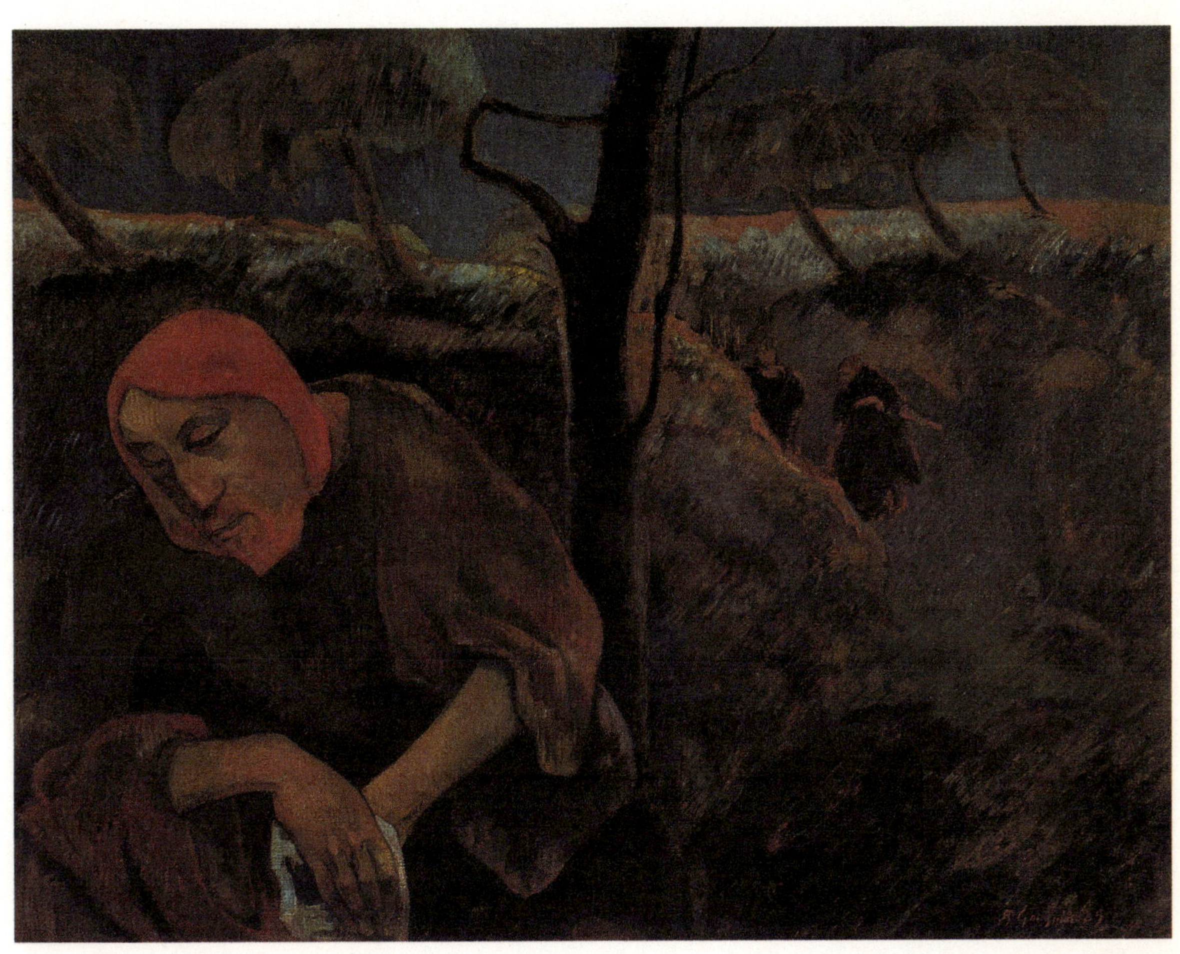

Christ in the Garden of Olives,
1889.
Oil on canvas, 73 × 92 cm.
Norton Gallery of Art, West
Palm Beach.

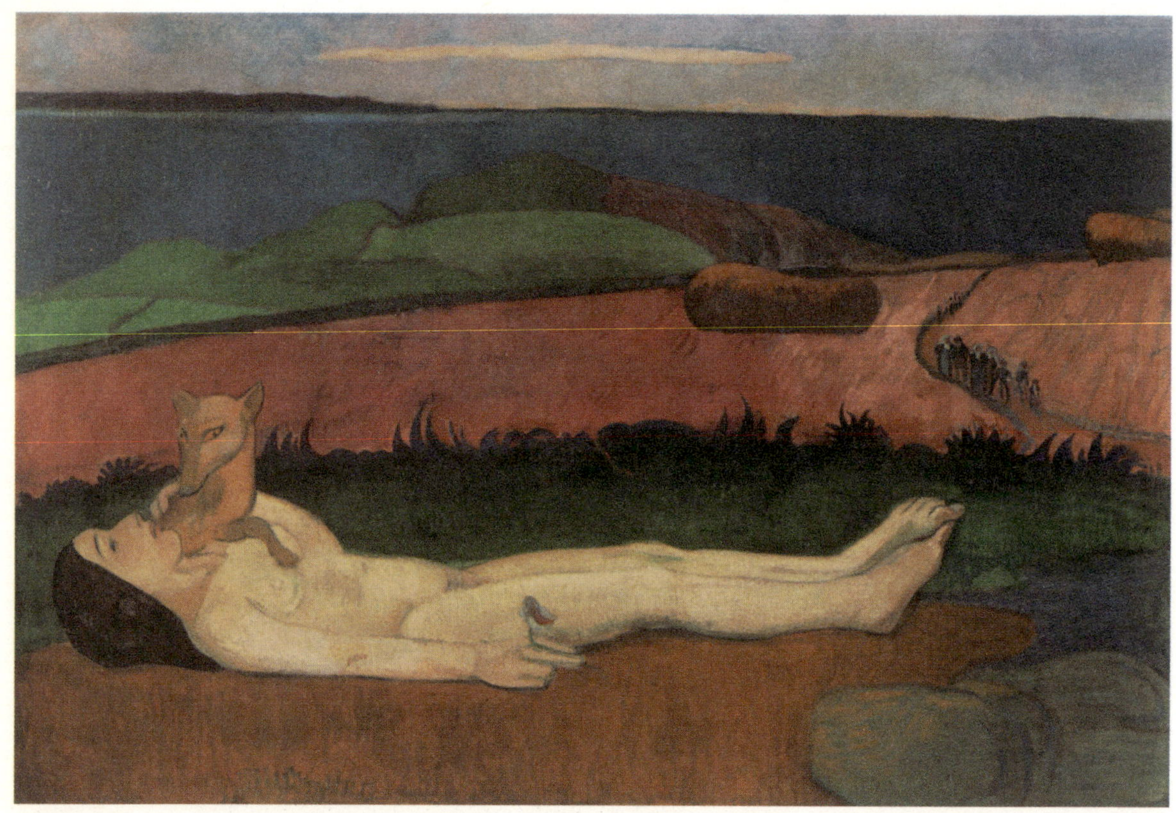

Loss of Virginity or Spring Awakening, 1890-1891.
Oil on canvas, 90 × 130 cm.
The Chrysler Museum, Norfolk.

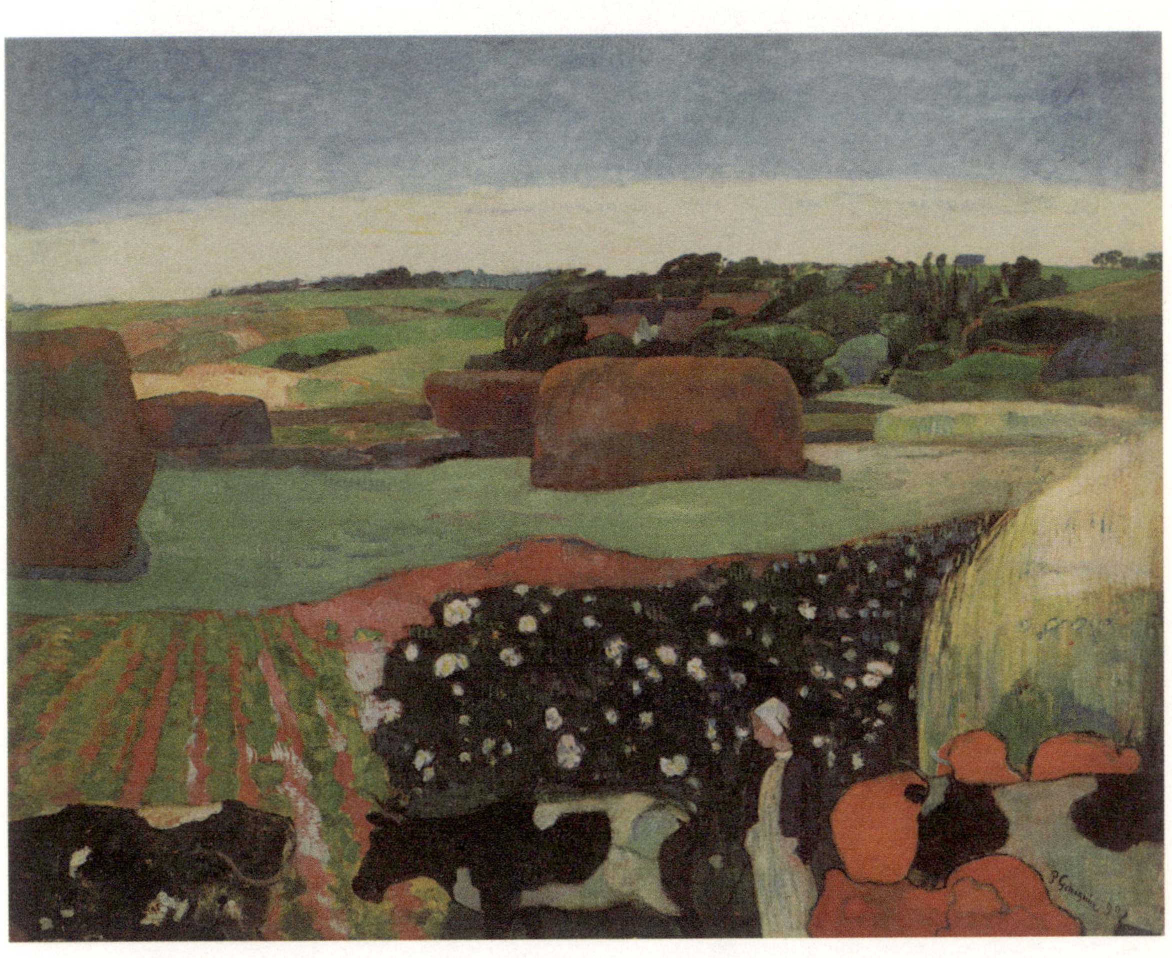

Haystacks in Brittany, 1890.
Oil on canvas, 73 × 92 cm.
National Gallery of Art,
Washington.

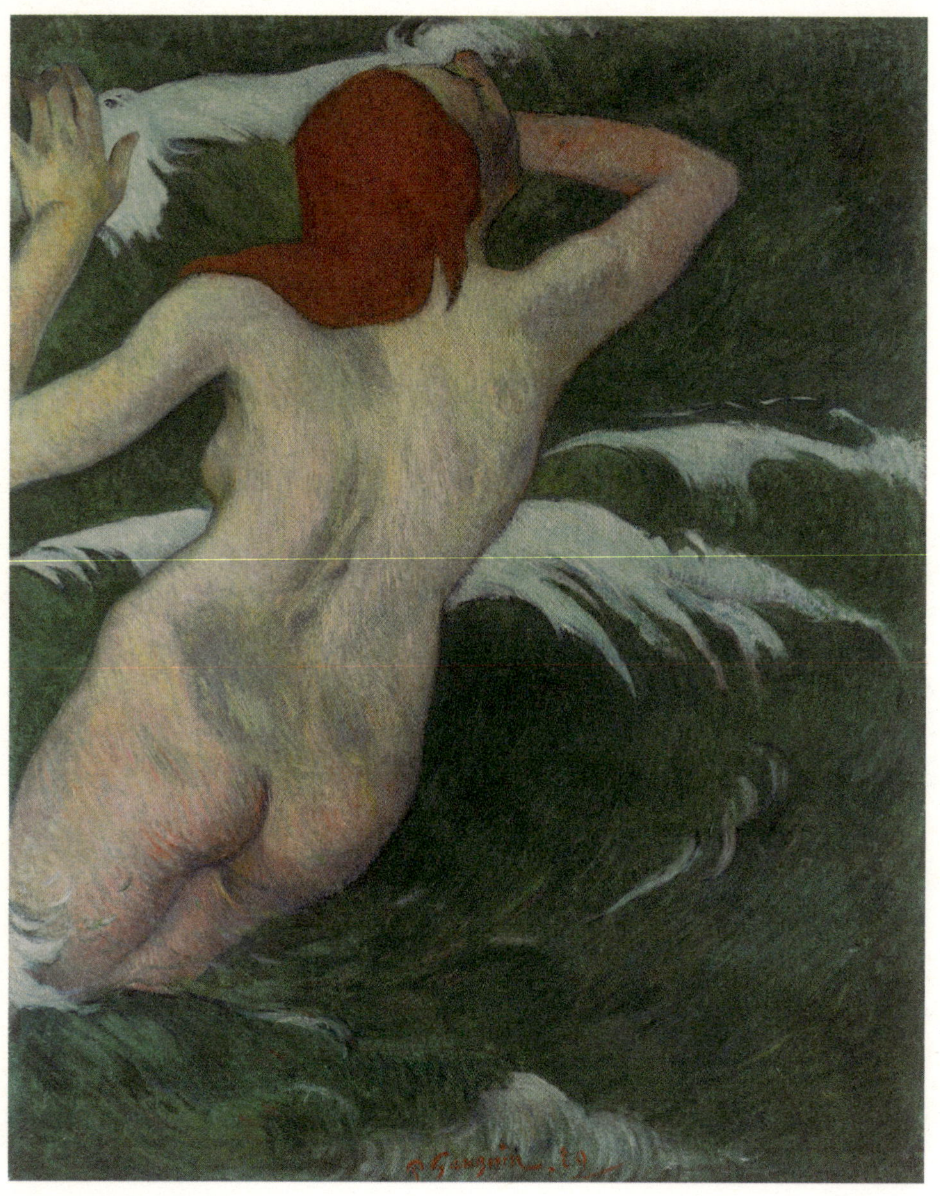

In the Waves, 1889.
Oil on canvas, 92 × 72 cm.
The Cleveland Museum of Art,
Cleveland.

in return only a frosty and perfunctory, "Bonjour M. Gauguin." Gauguin's exclusion from this particular indigenous culture in thus made clear. By 1890, he was resolved to leave Brittany and Paris for the distant colony of Tahiti.

Tropical Paradise. Gauguin departed from Paris for Tahiti in May 1891 in order to establish what he called a "Studio of the Tropics…where material life can be lived without money… and where living means singing and loving." There he would occupy a hut, he said, in a state of "primitiveness and savagery." Yet the circumstances of his departure from France and arrival in Papeete were not primitive. His passage was paid by the Colonial Ministry, and he possessed official letters of authorization and introduction. He was, in short, a colonist, intent on reviving his fortunes and finding fame in a distant land, beneath the fluttering French standard.

At first, he was well received by Governor Lacascade of Tahiti, and was even admitted in membership to the Military Circle, an officers club set in a tree house overlooking the largest park in town. For various reasons however—including the unconventional character of his Symbolist art and his sometimes boorish behavior—Gauguin's hopes to secure important and lucrative portrait commissions were quickly dashed. Soon thereafter, he retreated from the capital to Mataiea, a small town some 30 kilometers to the south, where he rented a little house that faced the bay and backed up against the hills and mountains. There he remained for nearly two years—sometimes in the company of his lover Teha'amana—devoting himself to representing the faces and bodies (they are not really portraits) of mostly unknown native women. His goal was to renounce his own colonial status, and to go native, or become *encanaque.*

Gauguin's paintings of women constitute the core of his Tahitian work. In *Les Parau parau,* (*Words, Words,* 1891) Gauguin spied upon a completely unremarkable scene of indigenous interchange and sociability, thereby rendering it noteworthy, historical and even ideal. The women in Gauguin's painting are engaging in conversation, or what a sexist Western culture dismissively calls gossip, keeping apprised of news, cementing familial or affective ties, castigating dissident elements in the community, and gaining knowledge of colonial politics. Gossip is a highly prized activity in Polynesian society, and "the coconut wireless" was an essential instrument in the struggles of native people to gain rights denied them by colonial authorities.

A similar transformation of the mundane into the historical is apparent in *Black Pigs* (1891). Here the un-naturalistically colored farm animals give the work a strange and even mythic character. (In Tahiti, the local pigs—*kune kune*—are mostly black and white.) The grazing horse at left is one of the many in Gauguin's oeuvre derived from animals in Arosa's photographs of the Trajan Column. The painting may also, however, be an instance of Gauguin's transformation of the historical into the everyday. The painting recalls the story of Circe from Book 10 of Homer's *Odyssey*, about the goddess living on the island of Aeaea who, with the help of a wand and some magical potion, turned Odysseus's crew into pigs. Odysseus himself however, forewarned of Circe's powers, managed to avoid the same fate. When the goddess discovered his cleverness, she restored Odysseus's men to their human form, and succeeded in persuading him to remain on the island as her lover. After a year, she even helped him to return home. The attraction of such a story to Gauguin—a sojourner to a distant Arcadia, a seeker of erotic pleasures, who nevertheless yearned for home—is obvious. Even the name of Circe's island closely resembles the Tahitian title of one of Gauguin's paintings, *Arearea* or *Joyousness* (1892).

Gauguin however transformed the grand water mansion built by the god Helios and the Oceanid Perse, into a pair of humble, thatched-roof houses set in a woodland clearing, occupied by a few women and animals. Circe may also be the inspiration for the figure of *Oviri*, accompa-

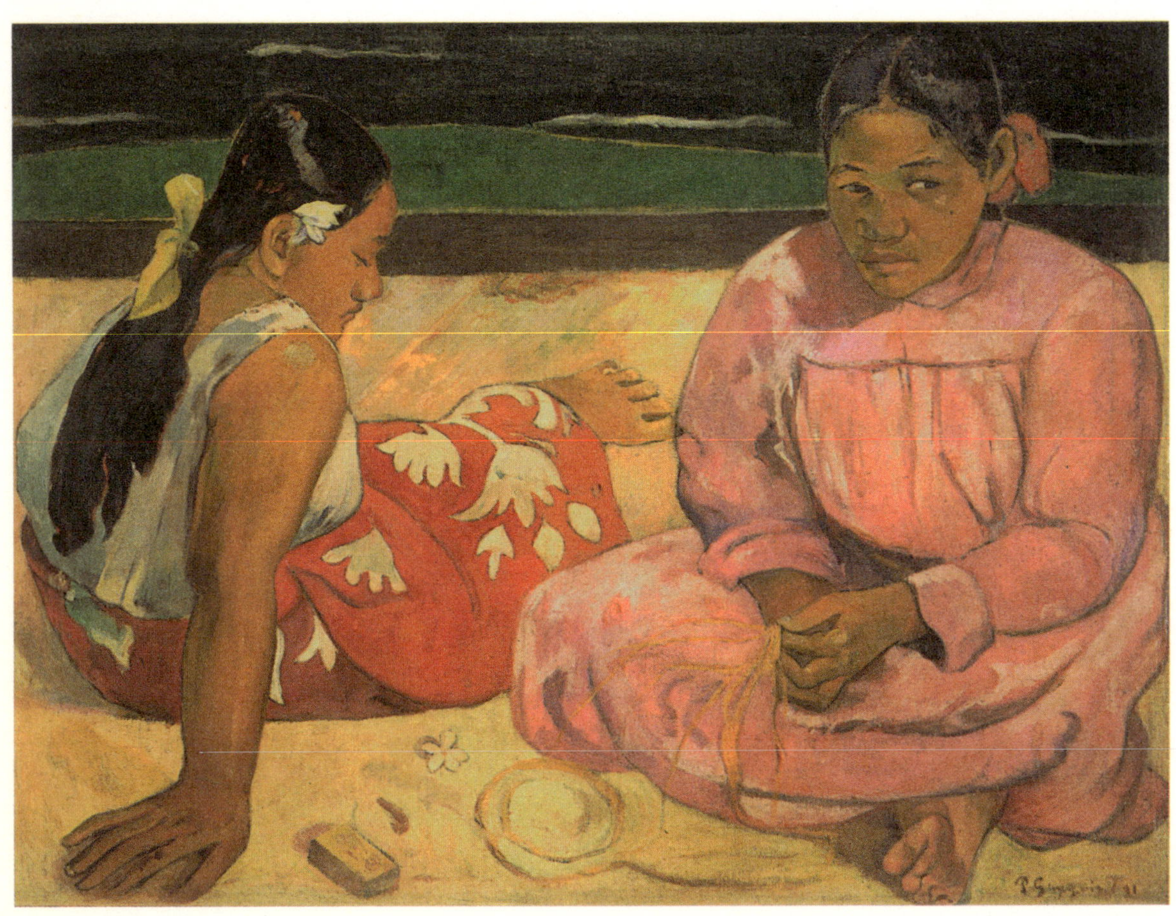

Tahitian Women or On the Beach, 1891.
Oil on fine canvas, 69 × 91 cm.
Musée d'Orsay, Paris.

nied by a creature at her hip who looks like nothing so much as a pig. The same figure, now given more naturalistic proportions, and again holding a black pig, is represented in *E haere oe ihia* or *Where are you going?* (1892). Indeed, the transformation from human into pig is explicitly the subject of a sheet from Gauguin's *Noa Noa* manuscript (fol. 35r), which represents the god Oro, changed from his human form into a black sow, accompanied by a number of other, smaller black piglets. In these images of metamorphoses, Gauguin is engaging ancient myth, Tahitian symbolism, European abstraction and every day reality in equal measure. For example, in Tahiti, pigs were for centuries important for food, ritual, gift exchange and even as pets. The sacrifice of a pig on the *marae* or temple grounds, might release spirits that could foretell the future, and the consumption of pork was sometimes the subject of ritual proscription, or *tapu*. Gauguin was at pains to learn about these practices and this history, claiming to have gained insight into Maohi ways from Teha'amana, though a more certain source was J.A. Moerenhout, whose *Voyage aux Iles du Grand Ocean* (1837) was partly transcribed by the artist, beginning in 1892, into his treatise *Ancien Culte mahorie*. This latter text was in turn a basis for Gauguin's famous diary/novel *Noa Noa*.

Many other of Gauguin's works engage this mixture of the mythic and the mundane. In *Manao tupapau* (*The Spirit of the Dead Watching*, 1892, p. 54), later made into a lithograph and several woodcuts, Gauguin represented a young native woman lying on her stomach on a bed, her feet crossed and her face directed at the spectator. She lies on yellow-white sheets shaded in green, blue and pink; below that is a bedspread or opened *pareu* with orange blossoms and leaves on an indigo field. Above and to the left is seen an ominous, hooded figure in profile. Gauguin described the picture in a letter to his wife Mette:

> I have painted a young girl in the nude. In this position a trifle more, and she becomes indecent. However I want it this way as the lines and movement interest me. So I make her look a little frightened. This fright must be excused if not explained in the character of a person, a Maohi. This people have by tradition a great fear of the dead. One of our young girls would be startled if surprised in such a posture. Not so a woman here.... Here endeth the little sermon, which will arm you against the critics when they bombard you with their malicious questions.[14]

Gauguin's painting did incite a few rude questions when it was exhibited in Paris two years later, and has continued to do so ever since. Indeed, in many respects, the work reiterates trite and sexist pictorial formulas dating back to the Renaissance. Supine and vulnerable nudes (sometimes accompanied by maids)—for example by Titian, Giorgione, Cranach, Velázquez, Rembrandt, Watteau, Boucher, Goya and Manet—constitute all by themselves a veritable history of European art. Moreover, contemporaneous Orientalist painting exhibited at the official Salons—for example *Slave Market* (1866) by J.-L. Gérôme—also featured non-white nude women available for possession or sale. Finally, the extreme youth of the figure, emphasized by Gauguin in his own account, makes it clear that she is to be viewed as weak and subservient.

But Gauguin's picture also strikes a number of dissonant chords that should cause us to question its place in the European tradition. Though the subject and composition of *Manao tupapau* derives from celebrated works by the artists listed above, it is also clearly indebted to the notorious antique marble *Hermaphrodite* in the Louvre. That un-canonical Hellenistic sculpture was the subject in 1863 of a poetic homage by Algernon Charles Swinburne that helped launch a school of

• • •

14 Maurice Malingue (ed.). *Lettres de Gauguin à sa femme et à ses amis*. Paris: Bernard Grasset, 1949, no. CXXIV.

"decadent" poets and artists whose psychologically intense and formally vivid works undermined the established hierarchies of lyric poetry and academic painting, and helped lead to the Symbolism of Aurier and Mallarmé. The conclusion of the third stanza of "Hermaphroditus" reads:

> Love stands upon thy left hand and thy right,
> Yet by no sunset and by no moonrise
> Shall make thee man and ease a woman's sighs
> Or make thee woman for a man's delight.
> To what strange end hath some strange god made fair
> The double blossom of two fruitless flowers?
> Hid love in all the folds of all thy hair,
> Fed thee on summers, watered thee with showers,
> Given all the gold that all the seasons wear
> To thee that art a thing of barren hours?[15]

Gauguin invokes with his painting a theme and subject remote from the canonized heterosexuality and anodyne classicism that is central to the Salon nude, represented by Cabanal's *Venus in the Waves* (1865) and Gérôme's *Slave Market*. Swinburne's poetical homage to the Louvre marble, in addition to Balzac's novel *Seraphita*, Gautier's *Mademoiselle de Maupin* and Baudelaire's condemned poem "Lesbos" are all sources and touchstones for Gauguin. Manet's debauched painting of *Olympia* was also frequently in the artist's thoughts in Tahiti—he owned and prominently displayed a reproduction of the painting, almost as if it were for him a talisman, and made a copy of it. Equally significant for the genesis of *Manao tupapau*, I believe, is Gauguin's actual knowledge (if not experience) of the sexual underground of Paris, where the community of Symbolists intersected the subculture of male homosexuals and cross-dressers, variously called *invertis*, *ephebes* and *insexuels*. In Tahiti, the merging of the sexes, dreamed by the artist's grandmother, the utopian socialist Flora Tristan, seemed to him a reality, or at least near at hand.

Metropolitan Interlude. In the summer of 1893, Gauguin returned to France in the hope of renewing ties to his friends and estranged family, and cashiering his new, exotic reputation. He quickly arranged with the dealer Paul Durand-Ruel to exhibit his Tahitian works, but was disappointed at the poor sales—only 11 of 44 works found buyers. And the exhibition received decidedly mixed reviews. There was considerable incomprehension—it didn't help that Gauguin insisted on using the Maohi titles—but the artist did receive favorable treatment from the Symbolist and anarchist press. Roger Marx described *Manao tupapau* as "a Polynesian Olympia," while the critic Achille Delaroch saw in it "all the mystery of the infinite." The Impressionist Camille Pissarro however was less sympathetic; his comments to his son Lucien reveal his anger and astonishment that Gauguin had essentially abandoned the world of the French avant-garde for the primitive spaces of Oceania:

> Gauguin is having an exhibition right now that is much admired by men of letters... The rest of us are baffled and perplexed. I've heard that some painters are unanimously of the opinion that this exotic art is too strongly cast in the Kanaka [indigenous] mold. Only Degas admires it; Monet, Renoir and company find it quite simply bad. I saw Gauguin, who expounded art theories at me and assured me that the future of the young lay in

• • •

15 Charles A. Swinburne, *Laus Veneris*. London and New York: Carleton and Moxon, 1866, p. 90.

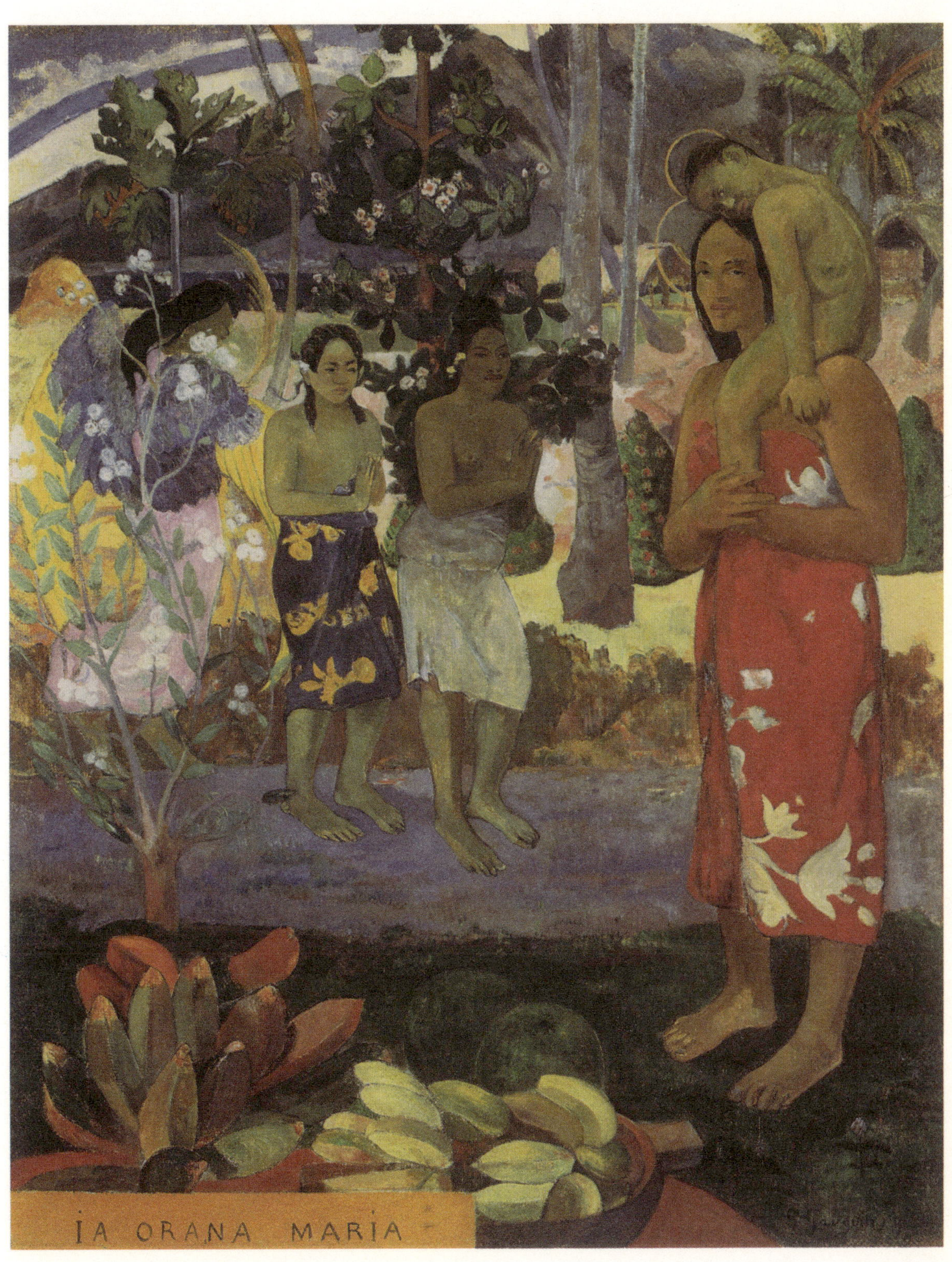

Ia Orana Maria (Hail Mary),
c. 1891-1892.
Oil on canvas, 113.7 × 91 cm.
The Metropolitan Museum of
Art, New York.

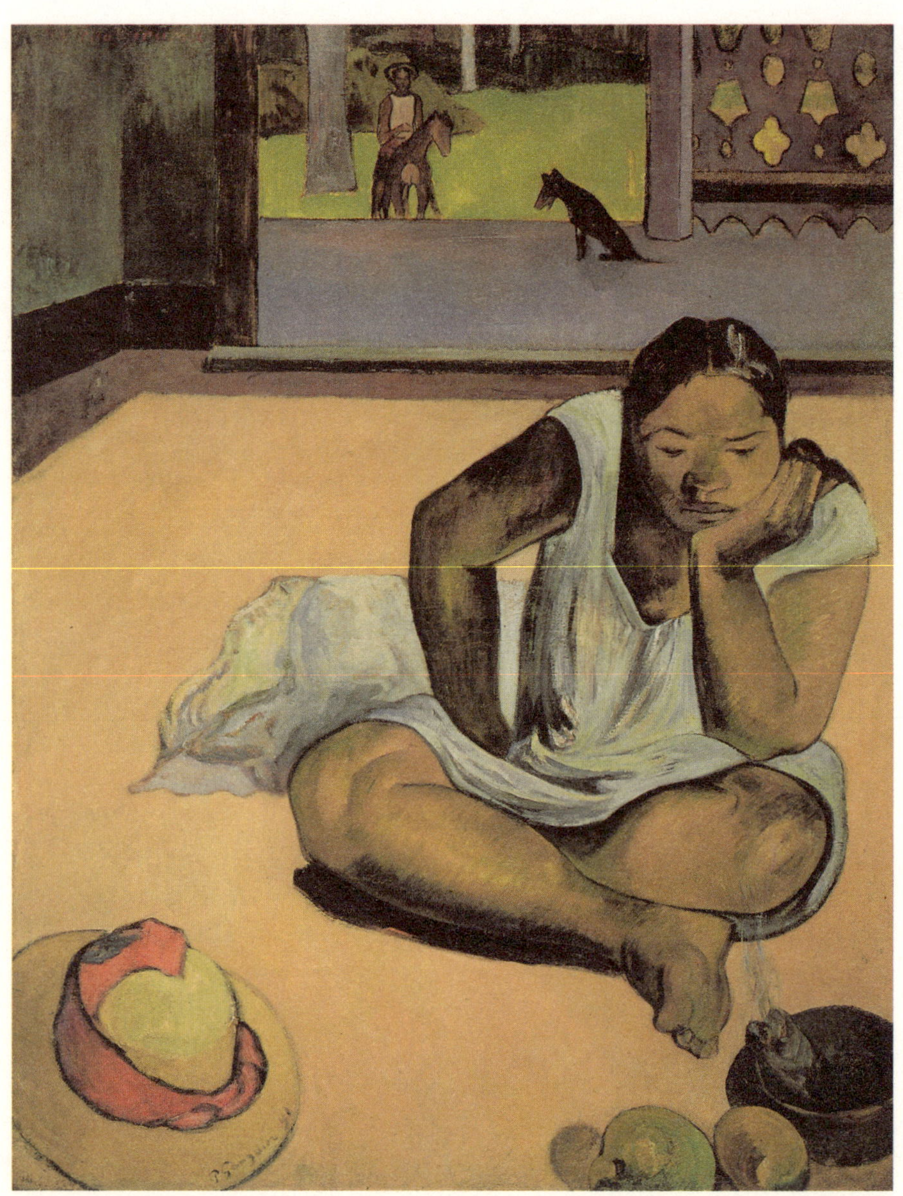

Te faaturuma (Brooding Woman),
1891.
Oil on fine canvas, 91 × 68 cm.
Worcester Art Museum.

> their replenishing themselves in these faraway sources! I told him that this art was not for him, that he was a civilized human being, and that therefore he ought to produce harmonious works....He is always poaching on other people's territories: today it is the turn of the savages in Oceania.[16]

Much of what Pissarro wrote was undoubtedly true. Gauguin was a "poacher;" like other French colonists, he wished to "replenish himself"—his masculinity, his imagination and his purse—at the expense of the Tahitians. Yet he also clearly aimed to set his sail by another, non-European, non-"civilized" culture. In so doing, he would criticize and help undermine the very notion of national schools of art, and even of the European tradition itself as a salient category. Gauguin's complex ambitions are most clearly summarized in his *Te rerioa (The Dream)*, and *Where do we come from? What are we? Where are we going?* (pp. 76-77) both completed in 1897, two years after his return to Tahiti.

Envisioning a Golden Age: *Te rerioa* and the "Large Painting". Gauguin's *Te rerioa* aka *The Dream* (1897, p. 73) represents his attempted mediation of material and spiritual realms. The title is a Tahitian archaism—the more common phrase is *moe moea*—but Gauguin nevertheless meant it to mean simply *le rêve*, as he told De Monfried in a letter of 1897: "All is a dream in this canvas, whether it be the child, the mother, the horseman in the path, or the dream of the painter." The setting of this scene of nurturance and desire is probably Gauguin's own actual studio or bedroom at Punaaia, made even more fantastic and other-worldly—with its predominant colors of bronze-green, yellow ocher, orange and vermillion—than it undoubtedly already was. The landscape in the background of the picture, and the grisaille figures at left and right (paintings within paintings), are windows into an alternative world of fecundity and erotic pleasure. *Te rerioa* is thus a reiteration of that ancient dream of harmony of the Cumaean sibyl, the fulfillment of which is found however, not in the remoteness of time but of space—in the mythic islands of Oceania. Gauguin however realized a still more disturbing and contradictory dream of harmony at about the same time.

In a letter from February 1898 addressed to his friend Daniel de Monfreid in Paris, Gauguin stated that his new "large painting" was conjured in his mind during the fervid hours after a failed suicide attempt. In the month that followed, he said, he worked like a demon to finish the painting: "I shall never do anything better, or even like it. Before death I put in it all my energy, a passion so dolorous, amid circumstances so terrible, and so clear was my vision that the haste of the execution is lost and life surges up. It doesn't stink of models, of technique, or of pretended rules." Gauguin's melodrama should probably be discounted as avant-garde self-promotion; the suicide attempt may never have happened, and the origin of *Where do we come from?...* may have been as prosaic as that of any other of his Tahitian works. But his lines to De Monfreid indicate the desire to rid himself of the apparatus of Salon painting: models, rules, deliberation and technique could all be sacrificed in the rush to find passion and expression. And Gauguin has indeed jettisoned academic procedure and even material reality in his large painting. To begin with, nearly every figure or group of figures occupies a different pictorial space: the pair of figures at the lower left occupy one plane; the adjacent child eating a piece of fruit a second; and the playful kittens still a third. A small, dark patch of ground supports the feet of the ambiguously sexed figure in the center, who reaches up to grasp a piece of fruit. Besides her/him, a bulky Amazon—derived from the Parthenon Dionysus and anticipating the brawny women in

• • •

16 Camille Pissarro, *Lettres à son fils Lucien*, edited by John Rewald. Paris: Albin Michel, 1950, no. 217.

Cézanne's series of *Large Bathers*—carves out her own space from the ambient, fecund landscape. At the upper right, two standing, whispering figures with long pink-orange gowns are enshrouded by a gray-black cloud; below them, two yellow-green women and a sleeping child just manage to constitute a discrete grouping of their own. At the far right of *D'où venons nous*, a hound gallops toward a dark figure with shoulder-length hair facing left; they cannot collide because like every other figure or animal, they occupy a different space or time. Indeed, the spatial ambiguities of the painting are compounded by carefully contrived chronological ambiguities. Unlike the rest of the canvas, the upper corners are painted with flat, glossy chrome-yellow upon which is inscribed the title of the work (left) and the name of the artist (right). It is thus treated "like a fresco," the artist wrote, "whose corners are spoiled with age, and which is appliqued upon a golden wall." What Gauguin has done here, in other words, is conceive his painting as if it were an old, partly ruined fresco that has been removed from one wall and reattached at a later date to a different wall! He intended to make a mural painting that was at once contemporary and historical, Tahitian and international.

Where do we come from? and the eight other canvases exhibited along side it at Vollard's gallery in 1898, invokes Byzantine mosaics, sculptures from the Parthenon, Caravaggio's episodic *The Seven Acts of Mercy* and Georges Seurat's similarly sized "manifesto picture," *A Sunday Afternoon on the Island of the Grande Jatte.* Their iconography is derived from Tahitian cosmogony, the Book of Genesis and Thomas Carlyle's *Sartor Resartus*, a text which Gauguin owned and showed lying on a table in his 1889 *Still-Life: Portrait of Jacob Meyer de Haan.* Like Gauguin's paintings, Carlyle's book considers the nature of appearance and reality, and the difference between daily-life and dream. In chapter eight, the Faustian protagonist, a philosopher named Teufelsdrockh, asks: "Who am I: what is this ME? A Voice, a Motion, an Appearance; some embodied, visualized idea in the Eternal mind?...but Whence? How? Whereto? The answer lies around, written in all colors and motions, uttered in all tones of jubilee and wail, in thousand-figured, thousand-voiced, harmonious nature." Gauguin's *Where do we come from?* is his effort to explore and understand his own complex social, political and geographical location. He was at once an apostle of the French imperium, and yet an outcast from that same order. He had inherited the tradition of classical art—its ambition, scale and allegorical weight—and yet he wished to cast it aside all of it, except its utopian, mythic, and dream-like elements; he had benefited from a patriarchal order that gave him undoubted prerogatives, and yet he found that system stifling. By the end of the 1890s, Gauguin was deeply alienated from France and its civilizing mission.

Anti-Imperialism, Exile and Shattered Illusions. What had brought Gauguin to the remote South Seas? What were the myths, and what were the dreams that motivated him? Though he claimed he traveled to Tahiti in order to enjoy artistic and sexual freedom and to escape the long reach of state and religious authority, his motives were undoubtedly still more multiple. He certainly hoped to live the high life in the French colonies, or the life of the libertine, like the he-goat or faun in *Nymphs and Satyr* by Bougereau. (Sexual avarice is repeatedly on evidence in the artist's letters and diaries.) He may also have wanted to find adventure in the Pacific, perhaps by participating in some punitive assault against recalcitrant natives. In fact he joined in such a raid on Ra'iatea in 1895—as an observer—and afterwards pronounced himself sickened by the spectacle.

Yet Gauguin's very social background—family history, artistic profession, political beliefs and Bohemian lifestyle—made ridiculous such imperialist ambitions. Indeed, political, financial and even erotic emancipation remained elusive for Gauguin in Polynesia; for the most part, he only discovered there—or created—new obstacles to pleasure, creativity and freedom of action. Not

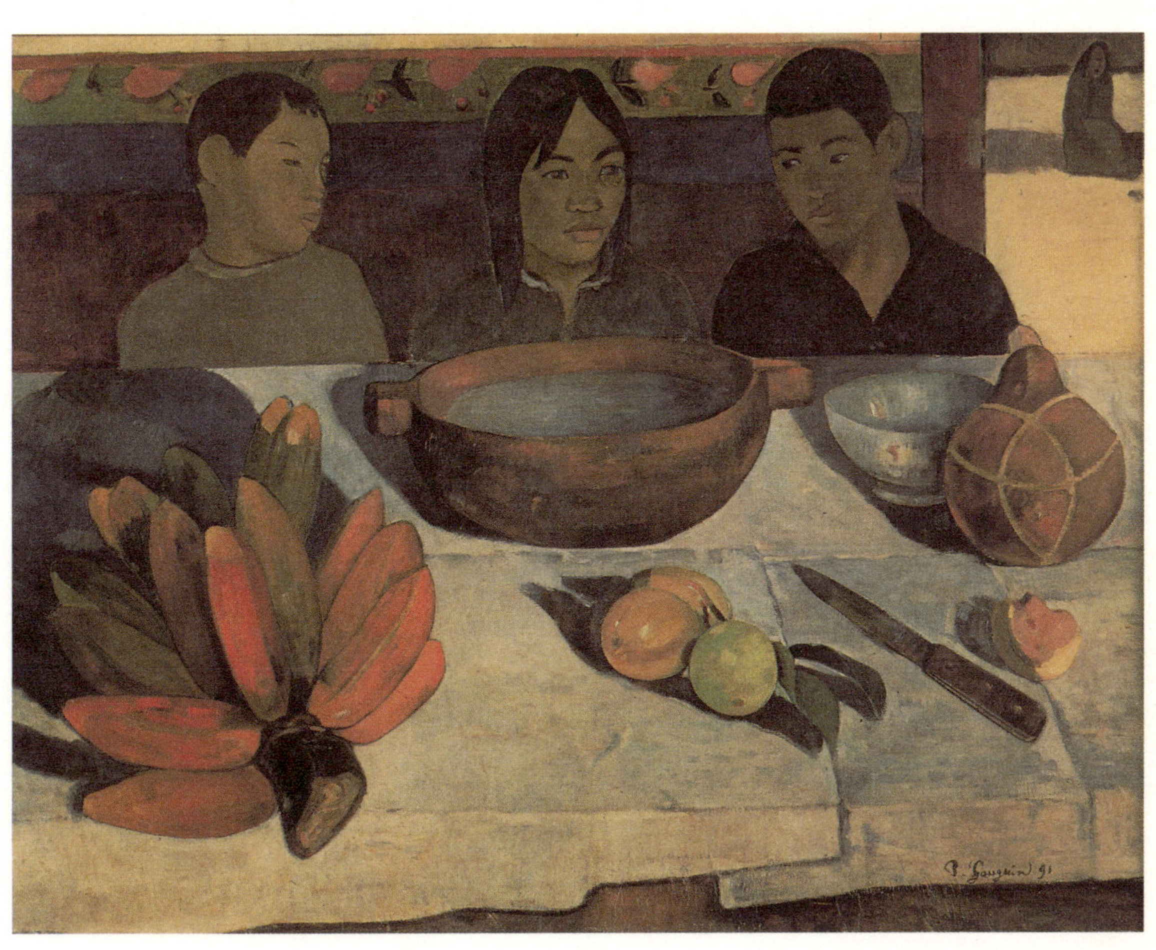

The Meal or *The Bananas*, 1891.
Oil on paper stuck to canvas,
73 × 92 cm.
Musée d'Orsay, Paris.

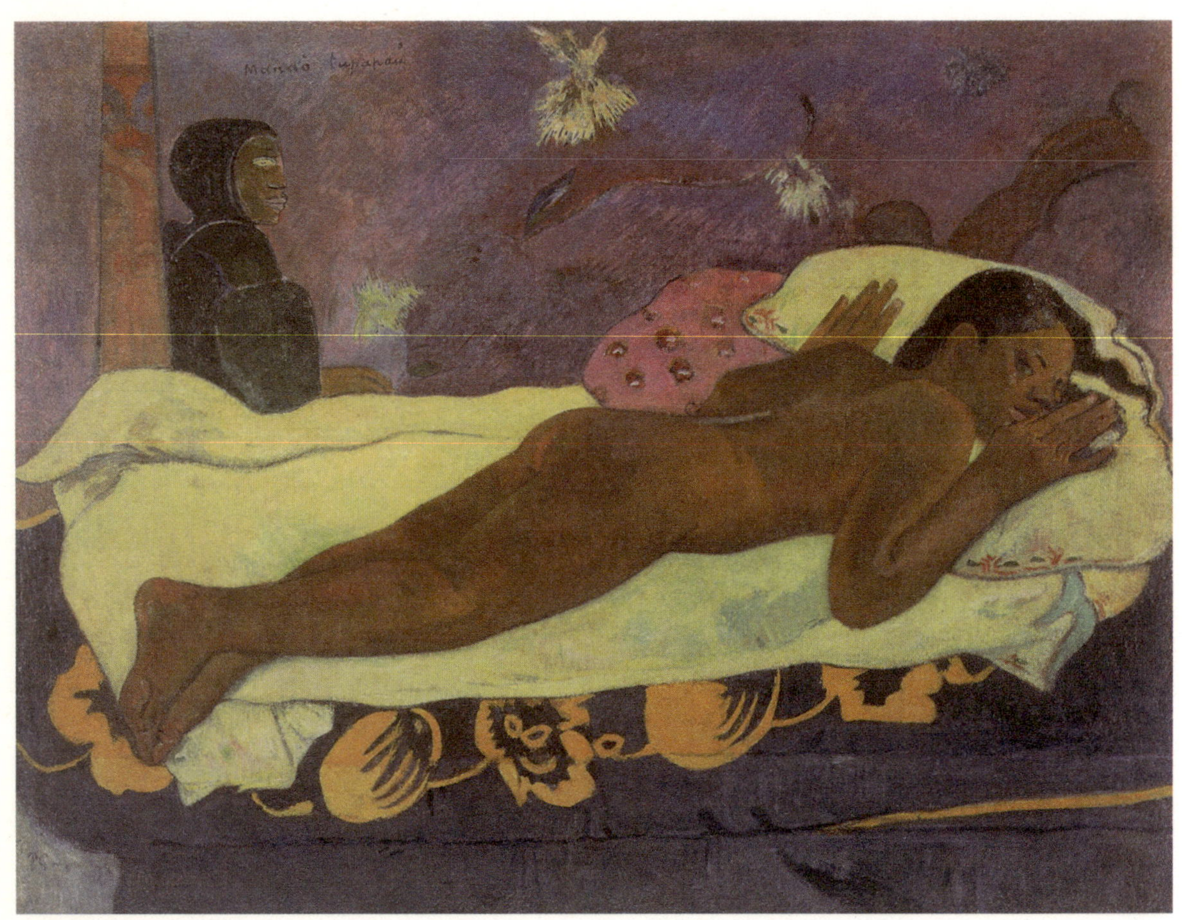

Manao Tupapau (The Spirit of the Dead Watching), 1892.
Oil on canvas, 73 × 92 cm.
Albright-Knox Art Gallery,
Buffalo, New York.

for Gauguin in the Pacific, as for Claude Monet at Giverny, a comfortable life in a big house in the countryside surrounded by splendid gardens tailor-made for painting. Not for him, as for Camille Pissarro at Pontoise, Eragny and Rouen, the respected roles of teacher, mentor and *pater familia*. Not for him, as for the decorated Salon painters Bougereau or Gérôme, a career of success piled upon success as an artist-entrepreneur following public taste. "Nail some indecency in plain sight over your door," Gauguin said in 1901 to justify his penchant for pornography, "[and] from that time forward you will be rid of respectable people, the most insupportable folk God has created." Now he would again refer to his own untamed, primitive, and satyr-like character in his *Head with Horns* (c. 1895-7), one of a series of late totem-like sculptures—some sober, some caricatural—that represent demonic and grotesque male figures. It is unclear whether Gauguin's perspective at this time should any longer be referred to as Virgilian, pastoral or Arcadian; it may rather be a darkened vision in which everyone and everything is in a fallen state. The *Head* is not that of a playful faun from Arcadia or mischievous pleasure seeker; it is instead closer to a head of Moses, the old Testament patriarch who literally laid down the law. "One's wife lost, and children disowning one. What do the wrongs matter? What does privation matter?" he wrote proudly in 1901, as he contemplated his growing isolation from family and friends. Gauguin clearly set out to violate bourgeois social norms, destroy hallowed artistic standards and create scandals wherever he went, and he succeeded. He aimed to be an agitator, a rebel, a stranger and a renegade, but also—when his will and his health permitted—to reconstitute by means of art, those dream pictures of a Golden Age that had preoccupied him since his first voyages around the world, when he was a young man in the Merchant Marines. Yet he was now compelled to look at Arcadia through a jaundiced eye; to notice its failures, contradictions and even its dangers.

Tahitian Idyll (1901) is just such a complex, dream picture; its tangle of palm and other trees, silhouetted against the orange and blue of sand and waves, recalls the artist's first, determined efforts to record Arcadia, the Martinique pictures from fifteen-years before, such as *Saint-Pierre Roadstead*. Here, Gauguin depicts a native Tahitian woman and child in the right middle-ground, a thatched long-house at right, some other thatch-roofed houses along the shore at left, and a schooner cutting through the waves in the background at left. The latter is perhaps a symbol of speed and the modernity that had, over time, disrupted the formerly gentle pace of island life, and upset the pastoral idyll. Was Gauguin also making a reference here to the exotic orient of Pierre Loti, (a.k.a. Julian Viaud), author not only of *The Marriage of Loti* (1880), a novel set in Tahiti and admired by both Gauguin and Van Gogh, but also *Madame Chrysantheme* (1888)? That novel concerns a French naval officer also named Loti who takes a young girl, O-kiku-san as his temporary wife, whom he quickly abandons after tiring of her. His departure by ship, her ocean of tears, and his sudden return (at which time he finds her counting money!), are key moments in the narrative. A few years after Gauguin's picture (1904), Giacomo Puccini and the librettists Luigi Illica and Giuseppe Giacosa, transformed the novel into the tragic *Madame Butterfly*. Here Cio-Cio-San and Lieutenant Pinkerton are presented much more sympathetically, and the latter's departure by naval ship and later return (with his new, American wife) are key, dramatic moments in the opera. Indeed, Gauguin's painting and Madame Butterfly are alike in another respect: both concern the interlocked matter of colonial and sexual exploitation, and the gulf of understanding between European (or Western) and Pacific peoples.

Unable to afford passage back to France, and uncertain that his artworks would ever find a ready market, he decided at last to make his exile more complete than it had ever been. In 1901, he sailed for Atuona in the Marquesas Islands. There Gauguin attempted to unite his art and his scandalously life. He built and decorated a new, native-style house—which he called "the House

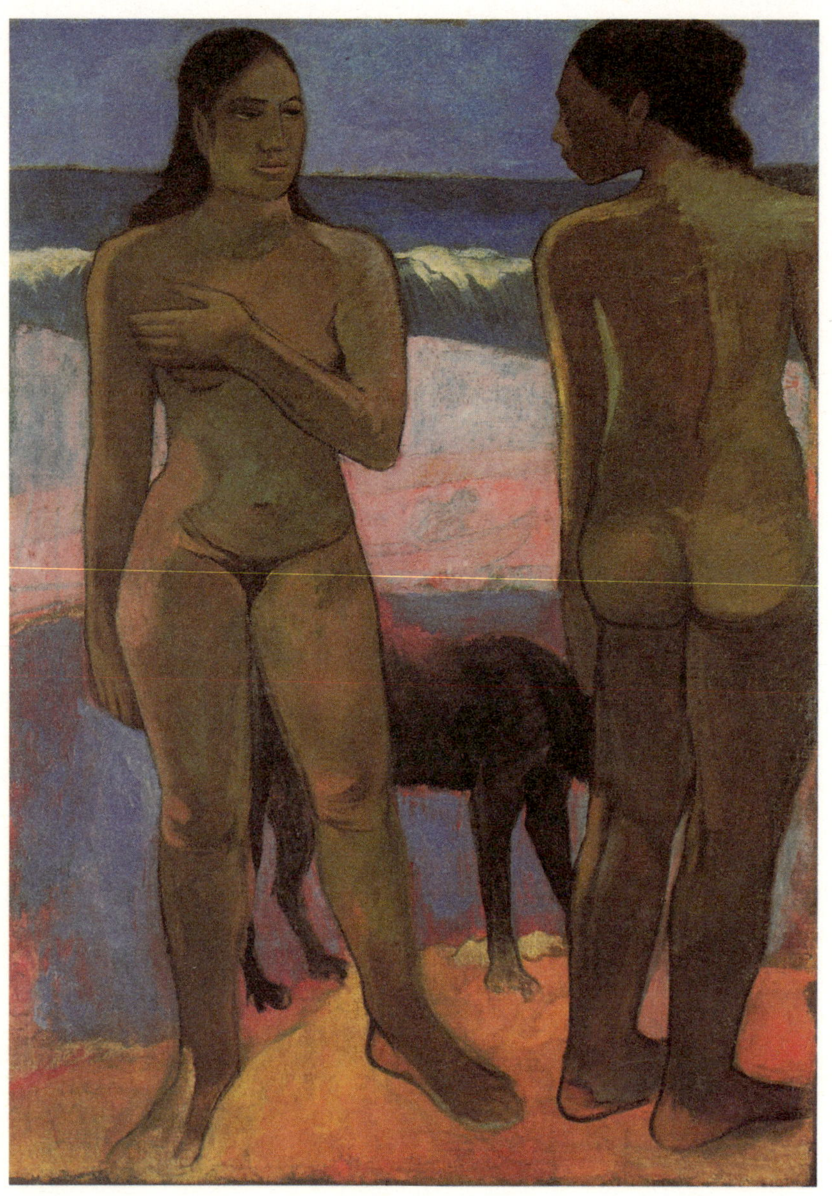

Two Nudes on a Tahitian Beach,
1892.
Oil on canvas, 91 × 64 cm.
Honolulu Academy of Arts,
Hawaii.

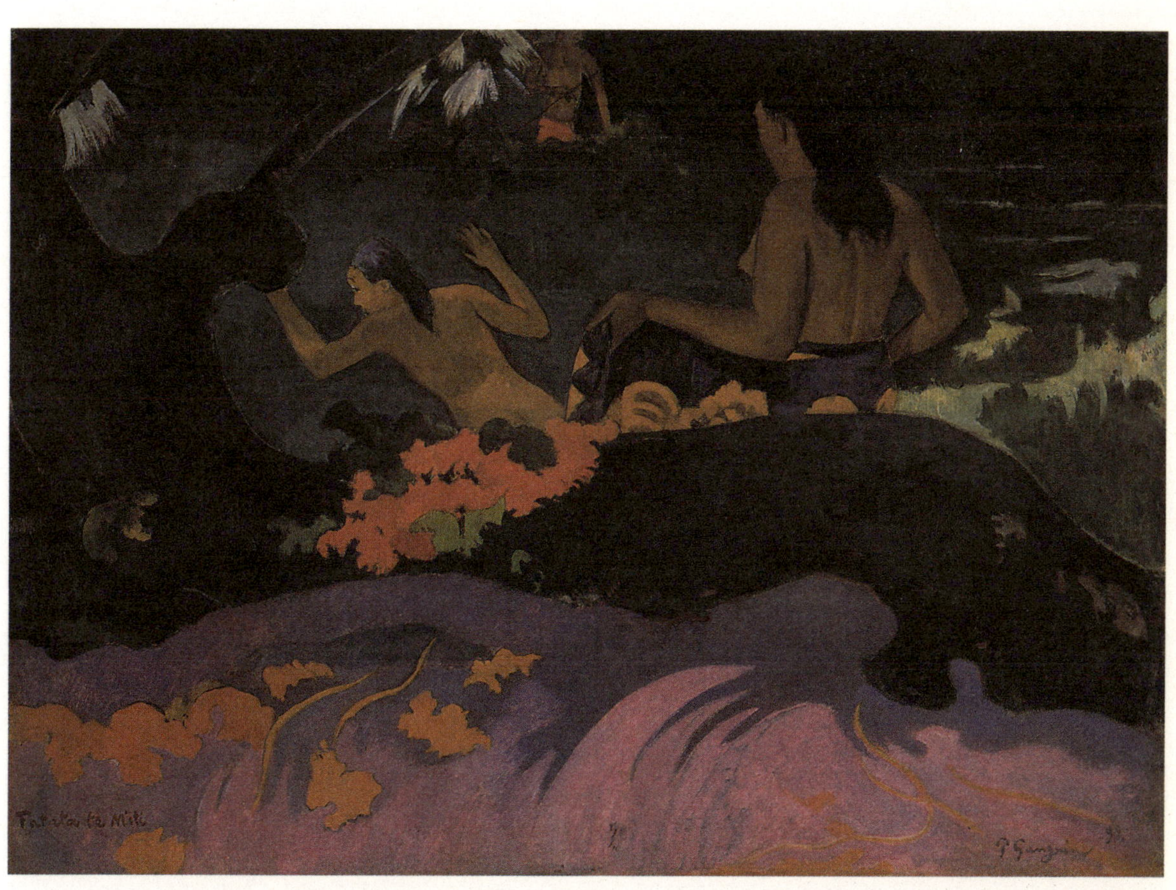

Fatata te miti (By the Sea), 1892.
Oil on canvas, 68 × 92 cm.
National Gallery of Art,
Washington.

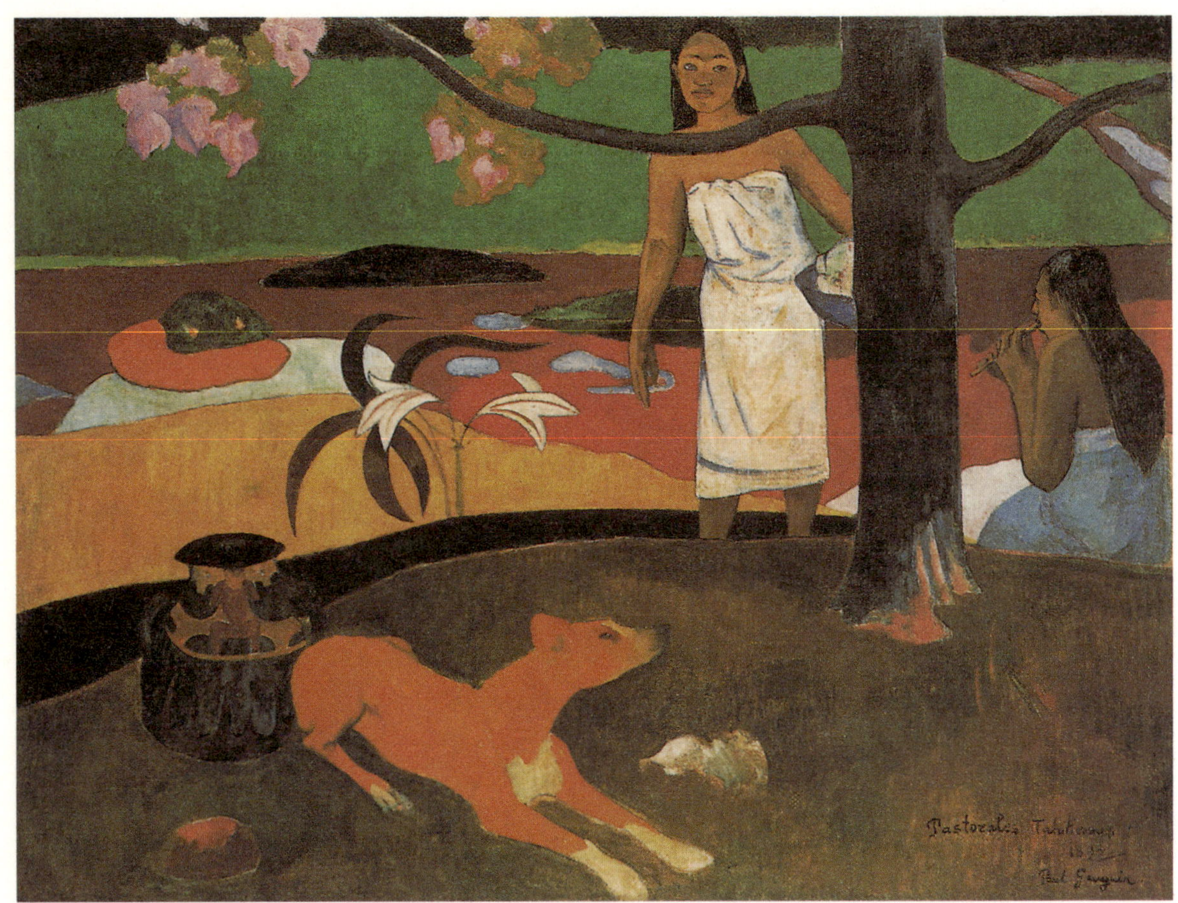

Tahitian Pastorals, 1892.
Oil on canvas, 87.5 × 113.7 cm.
State Hermitage Museu,
St. Petersburg.

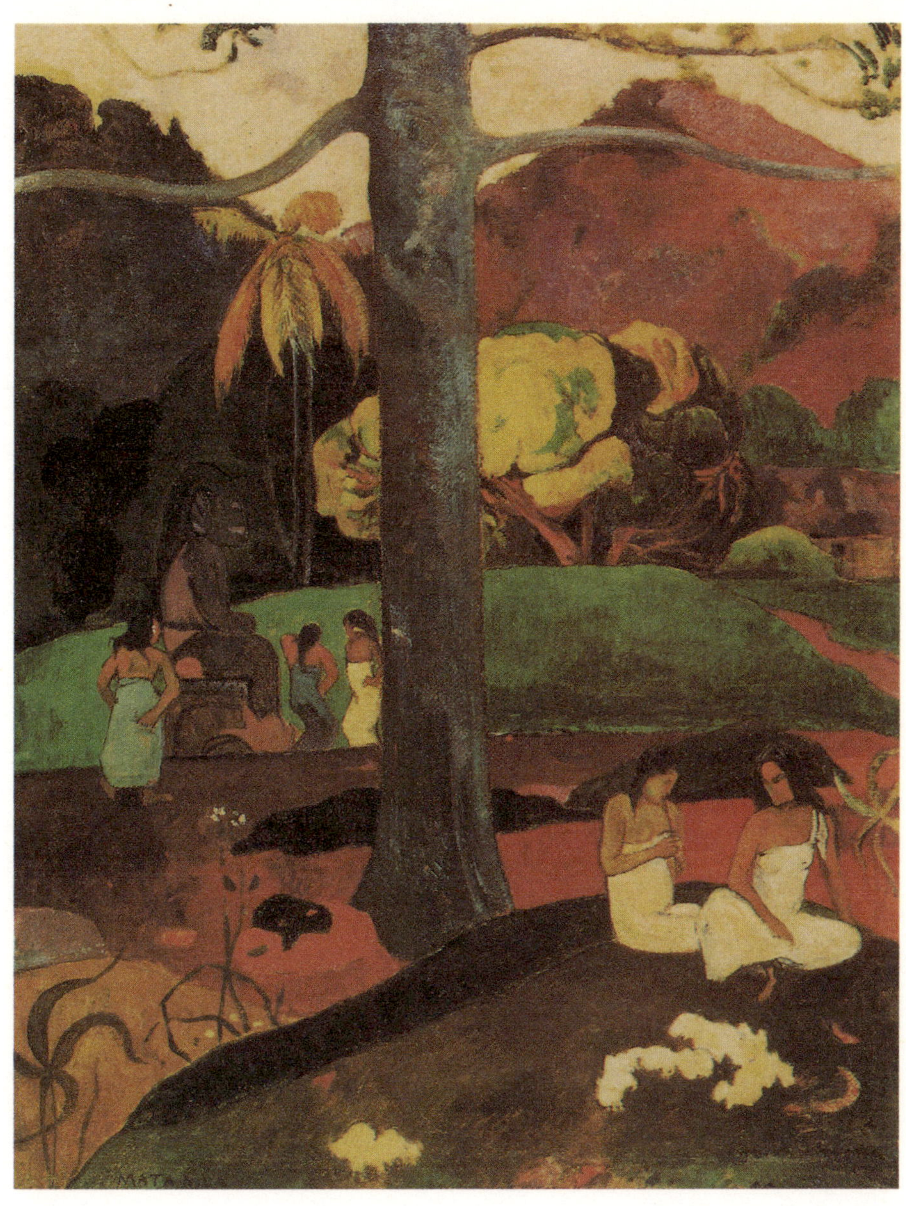

Mata Mua (In Olden Times),
1892.
Oil on canvas, 87.5 × 65.5 cm.
Thyssen-Bornemisza
Collection, Madrid.

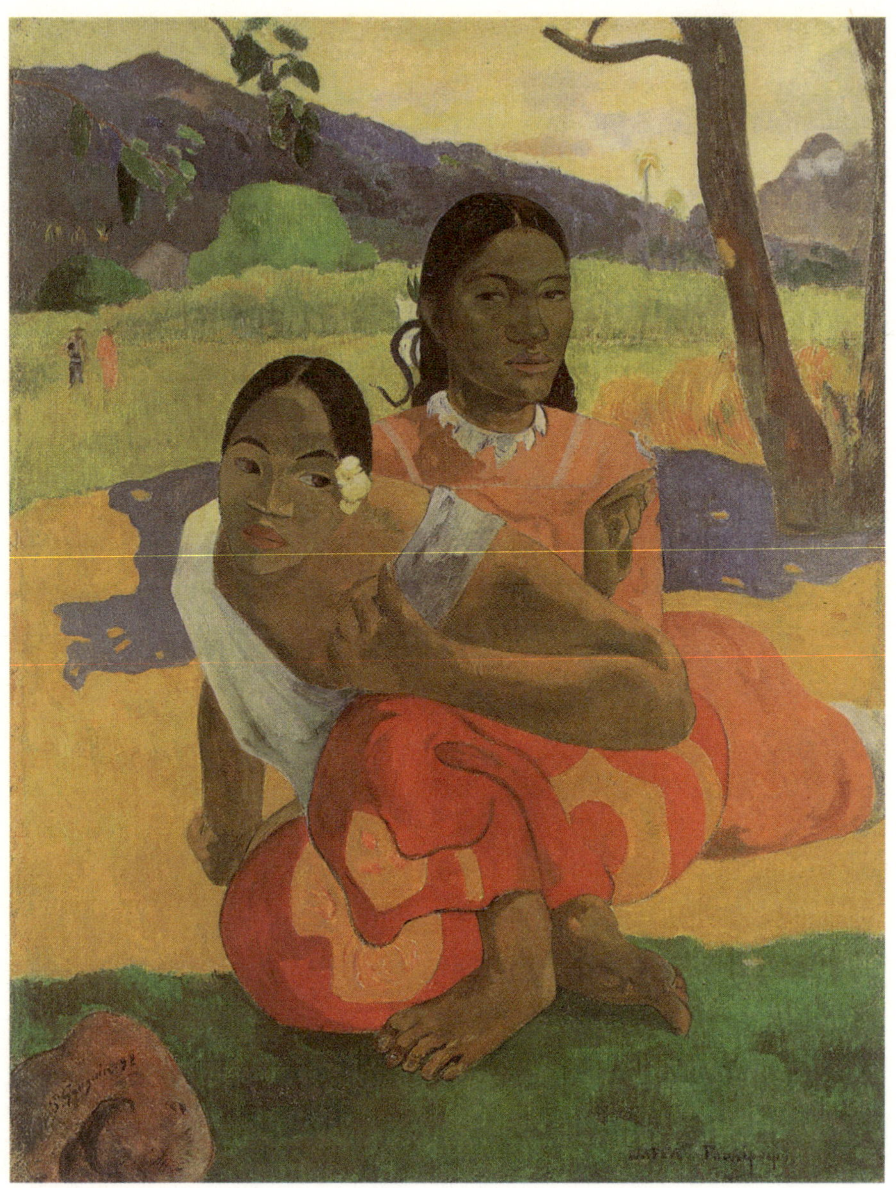

Nafea Faaipoipo (When Will You Marry?), 1892.
Oil on thick canvas, 105 × 77.5 cm.
Rudolf Staechelin Foundation, Switzerland.

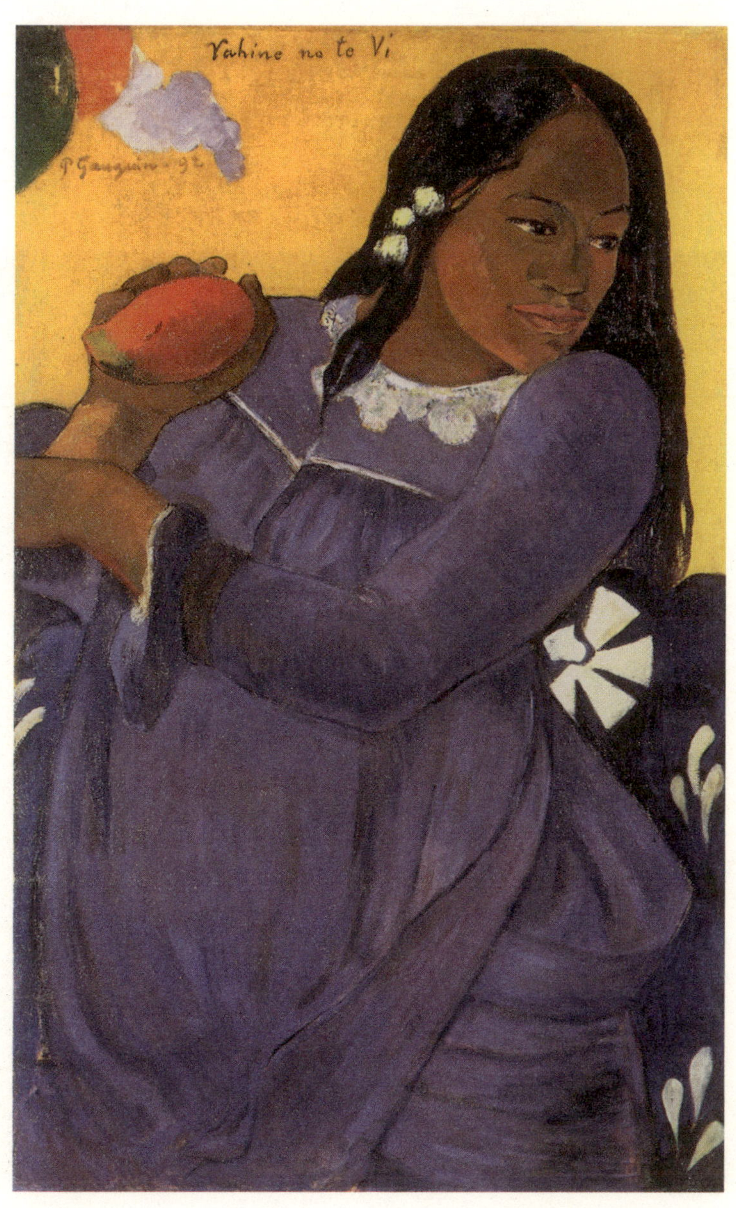

Vahine No Te Vi (Woman with a Mango), 1892.
Oil on canvas, 72.7 × 44.5 cm.
Baltimore Museum of Art,
Baltimore.

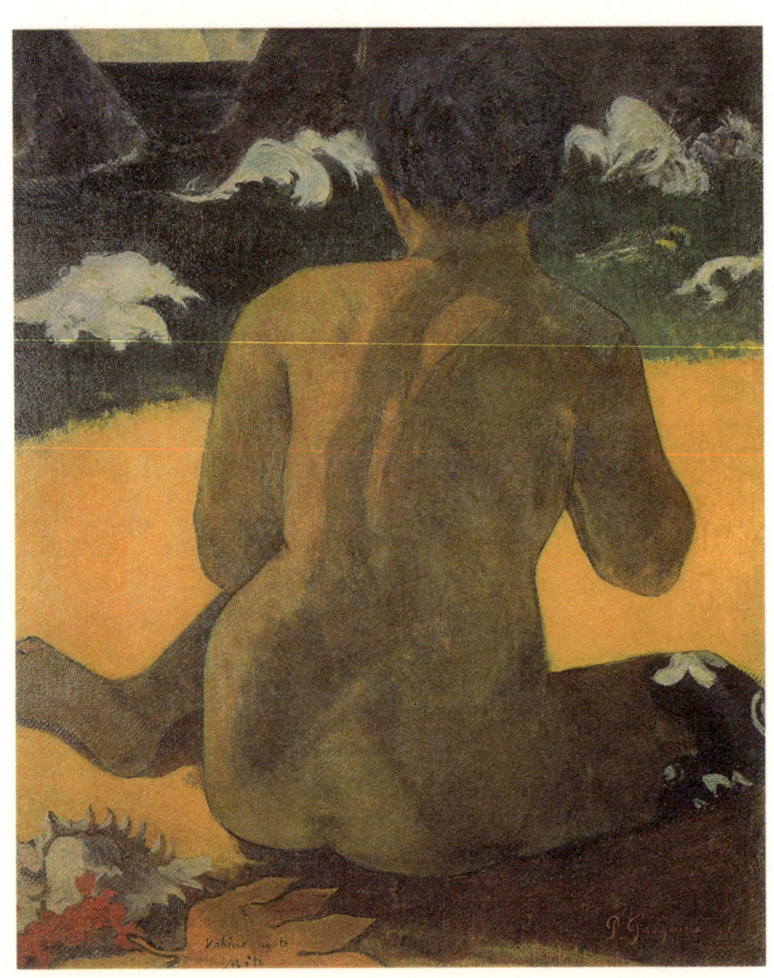

Vahine No Te Miti (Woman by the Sea), 1892.
Oil on thick canvas,
93 × 74.5 cm.
Museo Nacional de Bellas Artes, Buenos Aires.

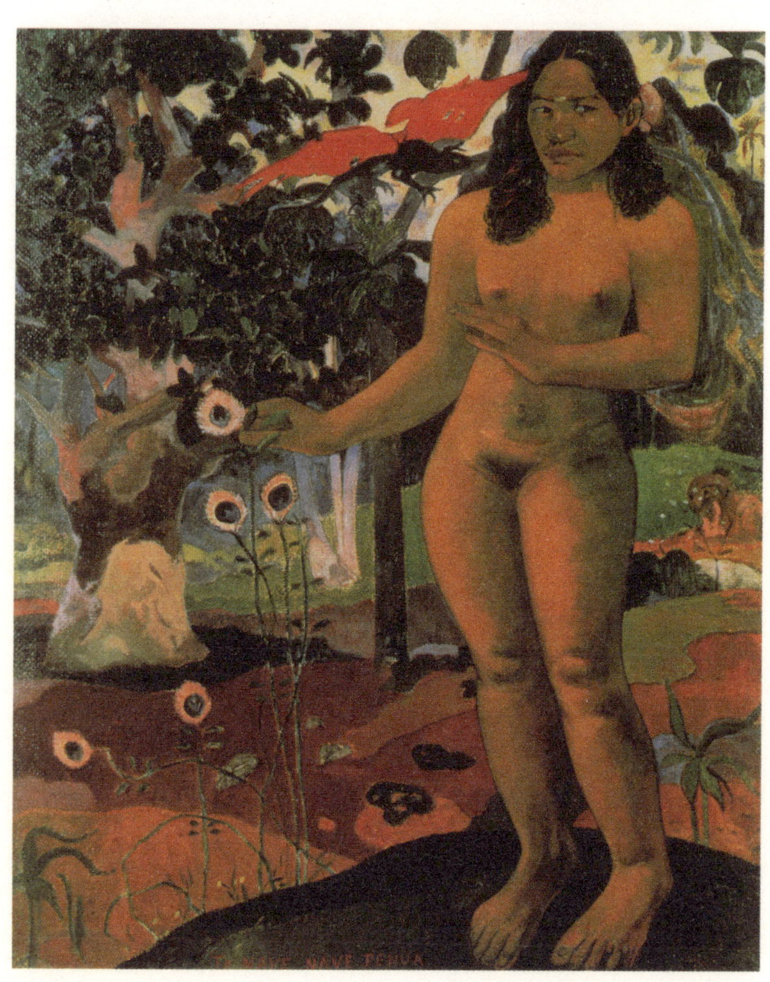

Te nave nave fenua (The Delightful Land), 1892.
Oil on thick canvas, 91 × 72 cm.
Ohara Museum of Art,
Kurashiki.

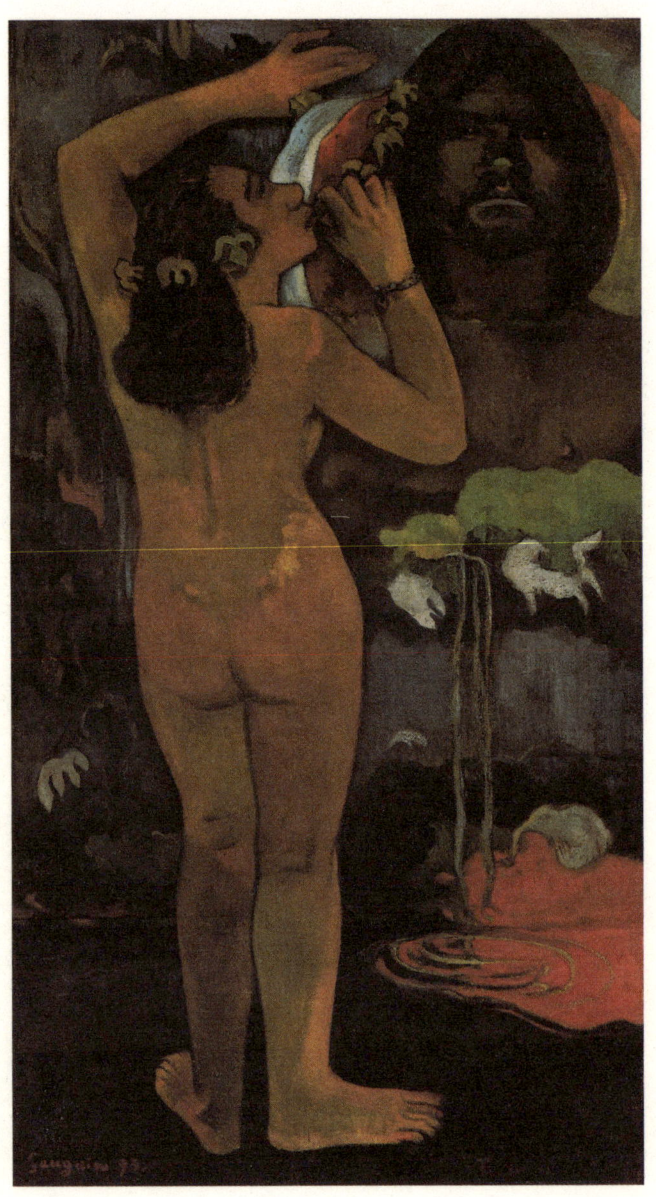

Hina te Fatou (The Moon and the Earth), 1893.
Oil on canvas, 114.3 × 62.2 cm.
The Museum of Modern Art, New York.

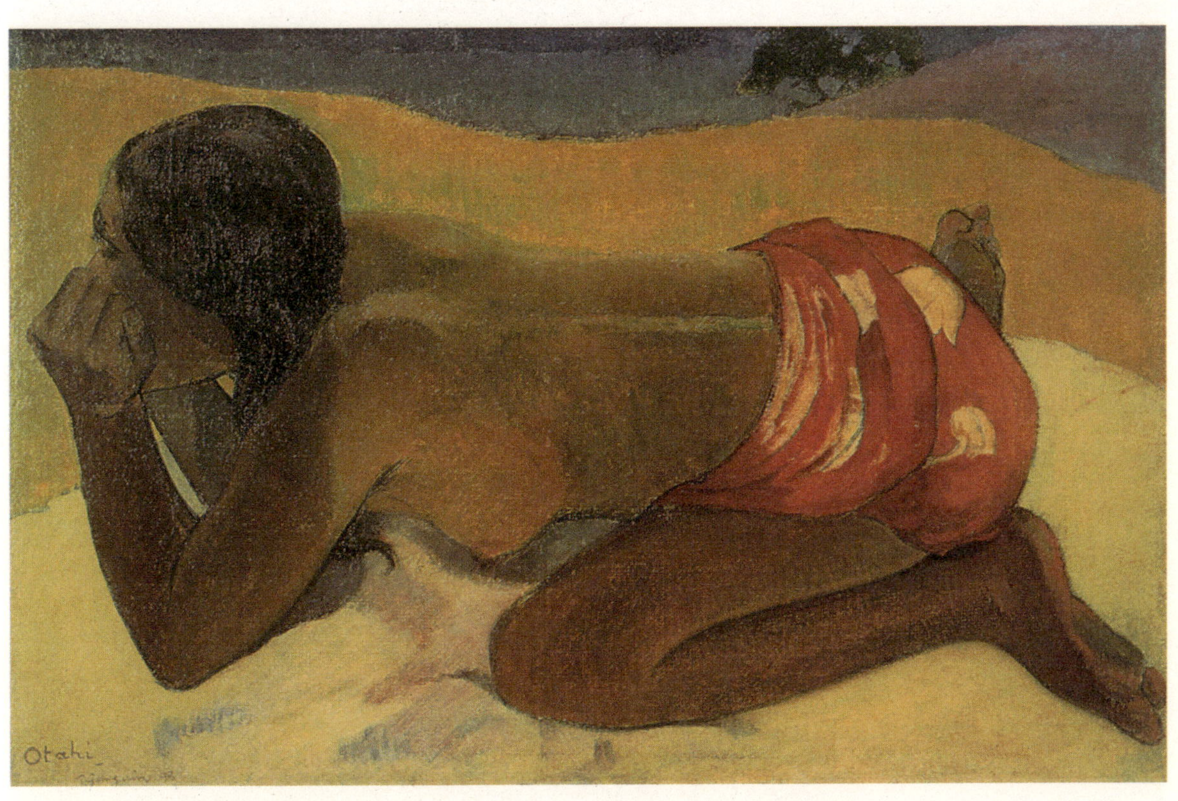

Otahi (Alone), 1893.
Oil on thick canvas, 50 × 73 cm.
Private Collection.

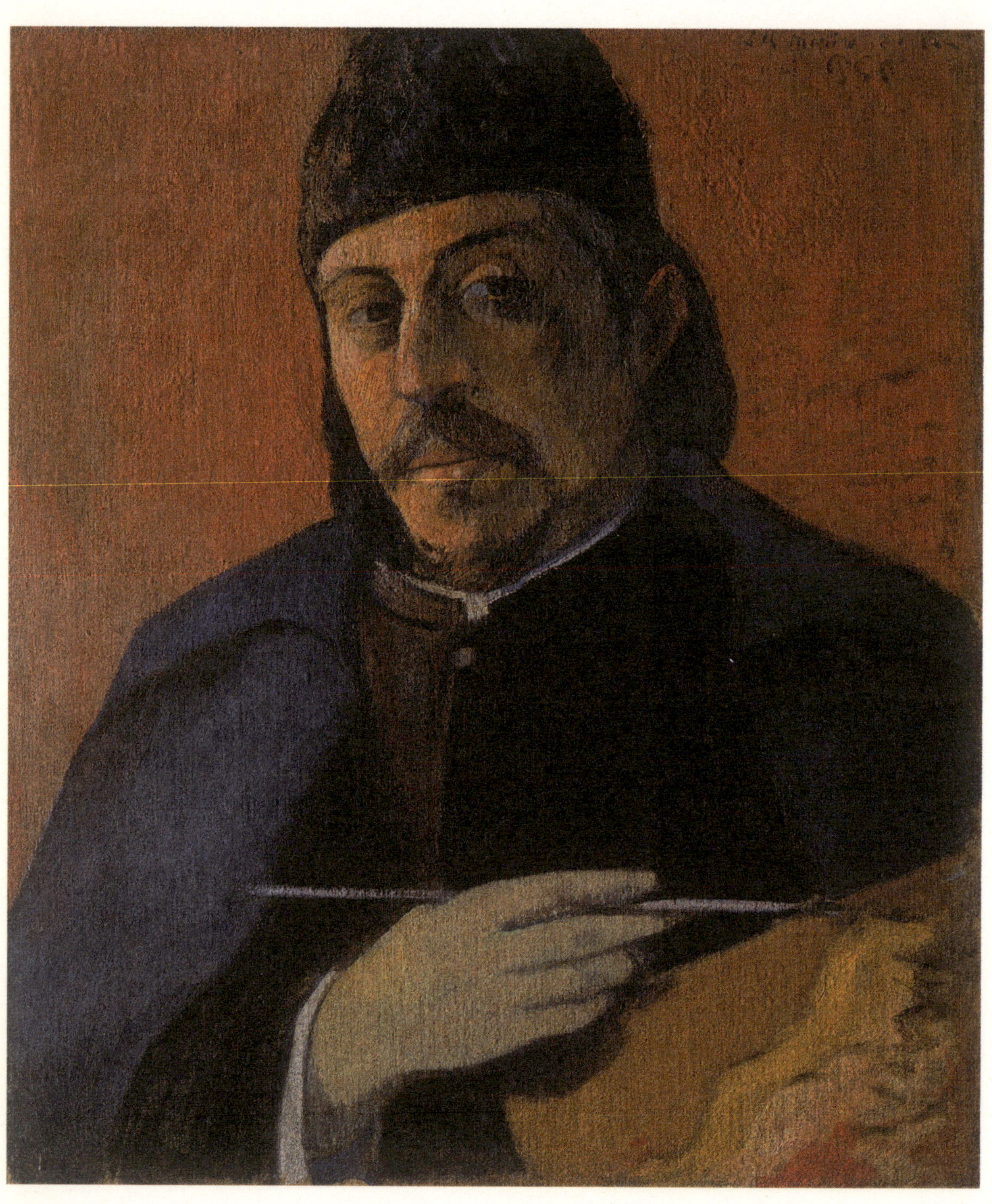

Self-Portrait with Palette,
c. 1894.
Oil on canvas, 92 × 73 cm.
Private Collection.

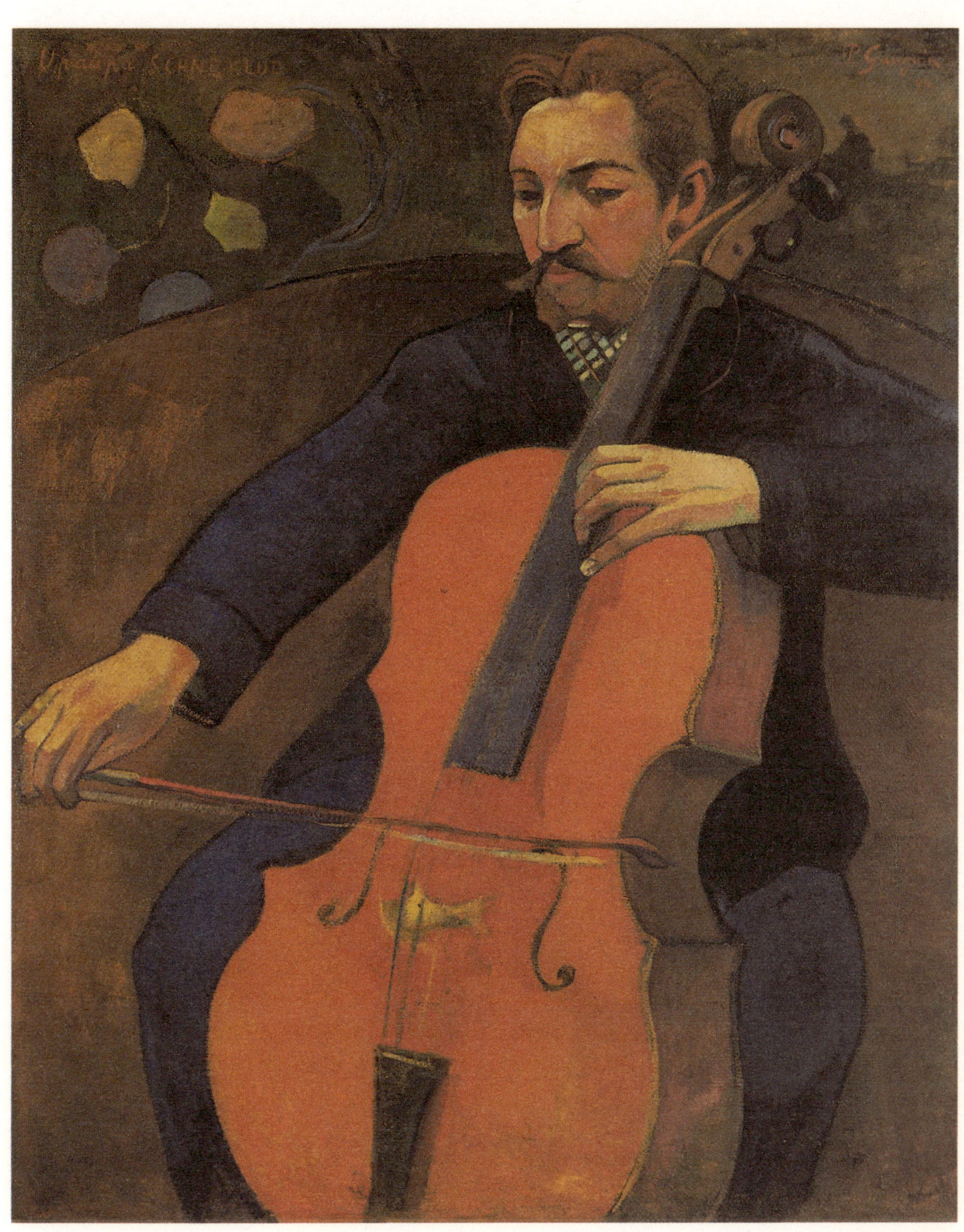

Upaupa Schneklud (The Player Schneklud), 1894.
Oil on canvas, 92.5 × 73.5 cm.
Baltimore Museum of Art, Baltimore.

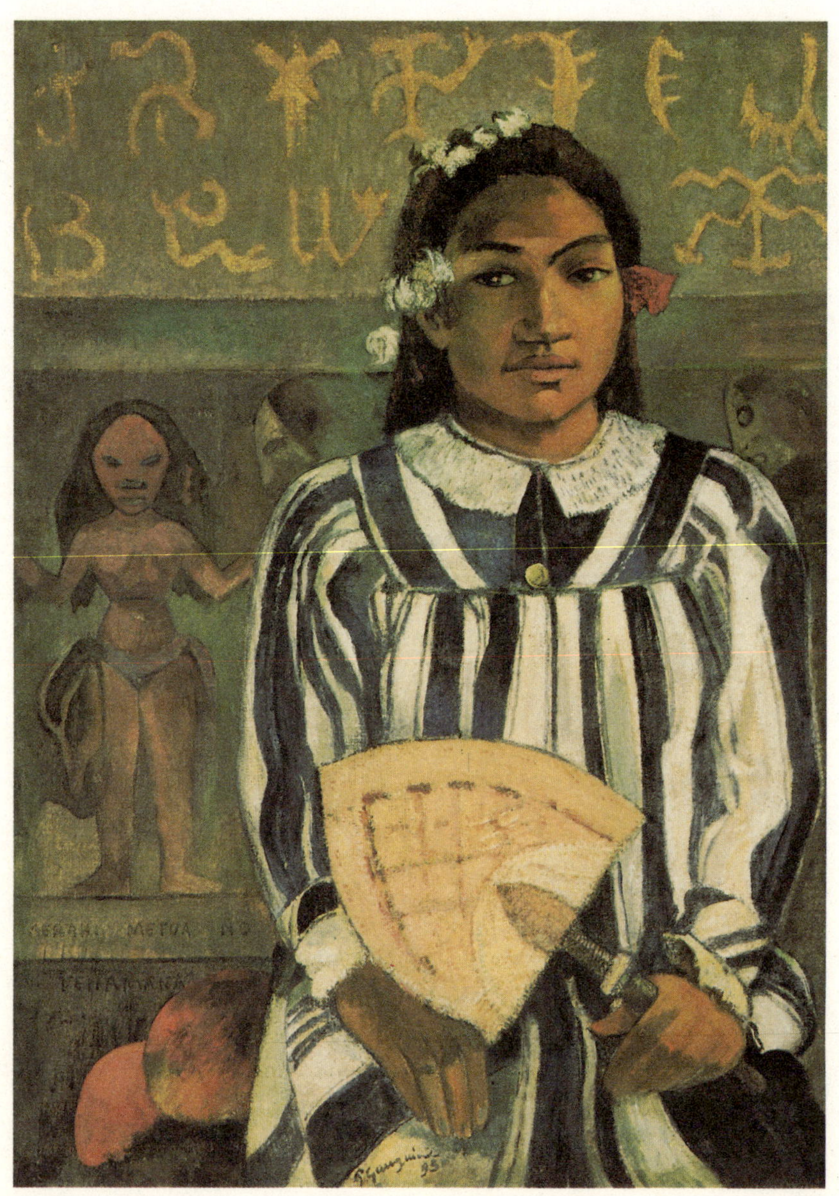

Merahi metua no Tehamana
(Ancestors of Tehamana), 1893.
Oil on canvas, 76.3 × 54.3 cm.
The Art Institute of Chicago,
Chicago.

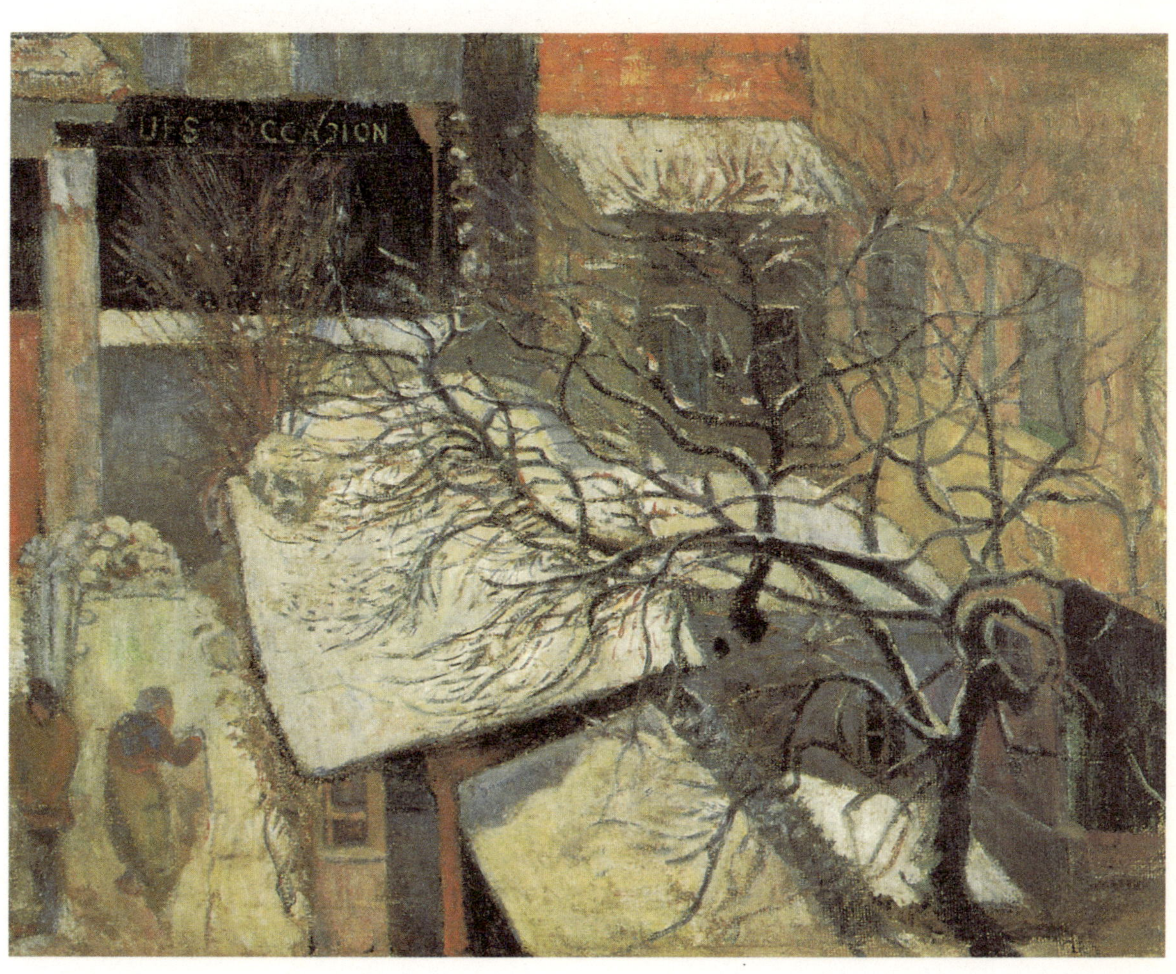

Paris in the Snow, 1894.
Oil on canvas, 71.5 × 88 cm.
Rijksmuseum Vincent van Gogh,
Amsterdam.

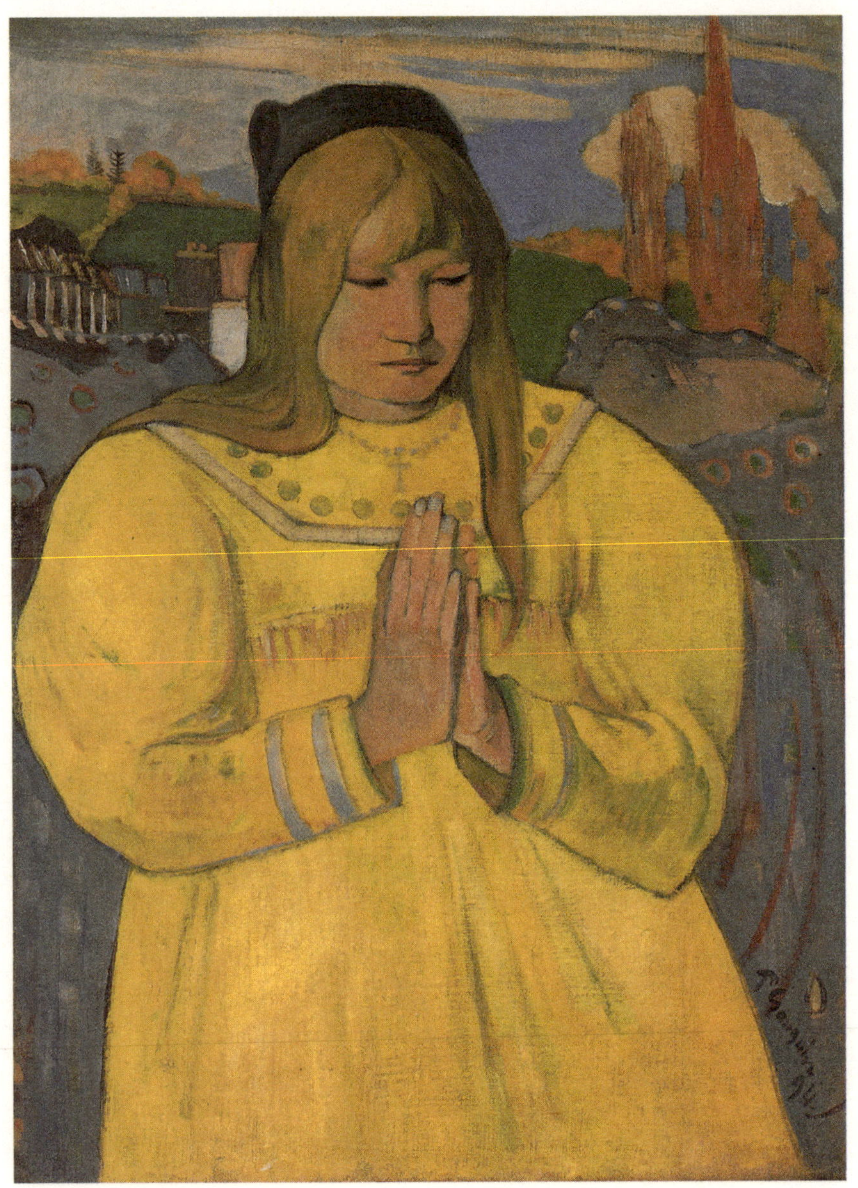

Young Christian Girl, 1894.
Oil on canvas, 65 × 46 cm.
Sterling and Francine Clark
Art Institute, Williamstown,
Massachusetts.

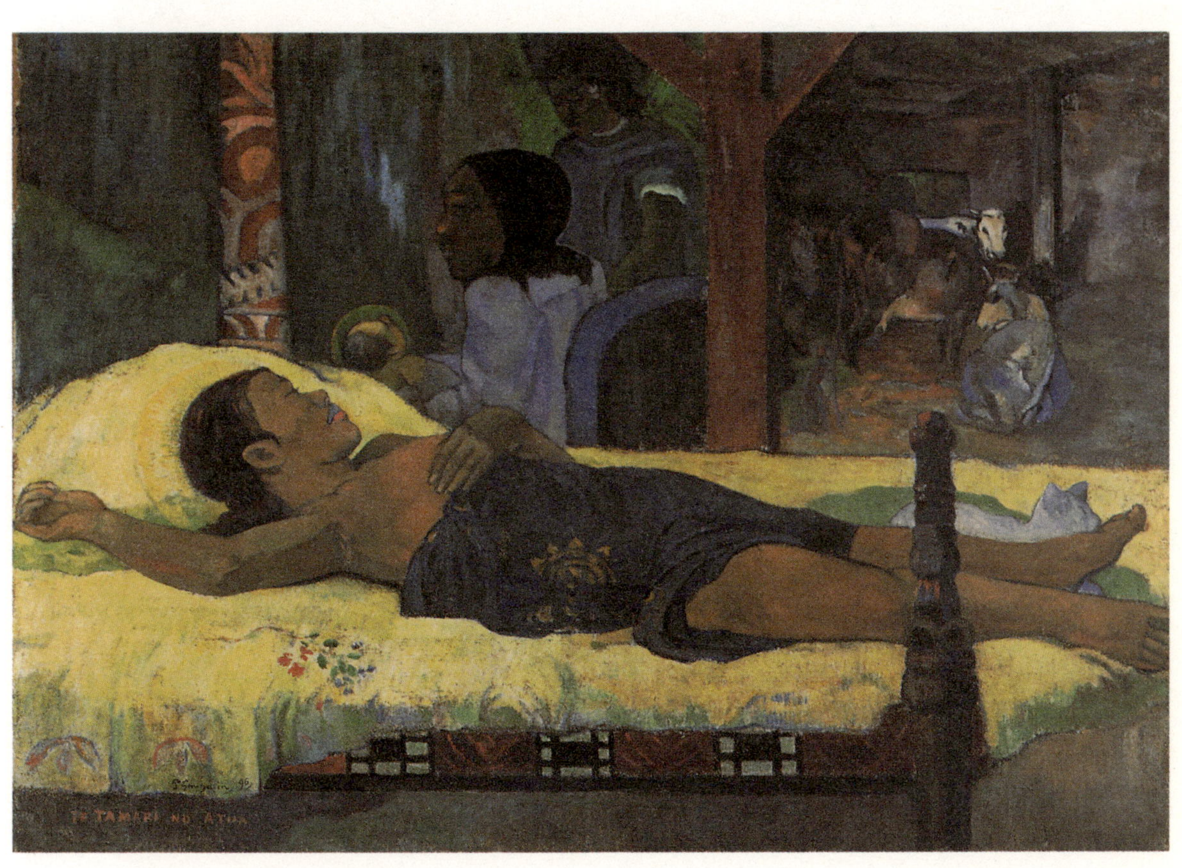

Te Tamari No Atua (Birth of Christ Son of God), 1895-1896. Oil on canvas, 96 × 128 cm. Bayerische Staatsgemäldesammlungen, Neue Pinakothek, Munich.

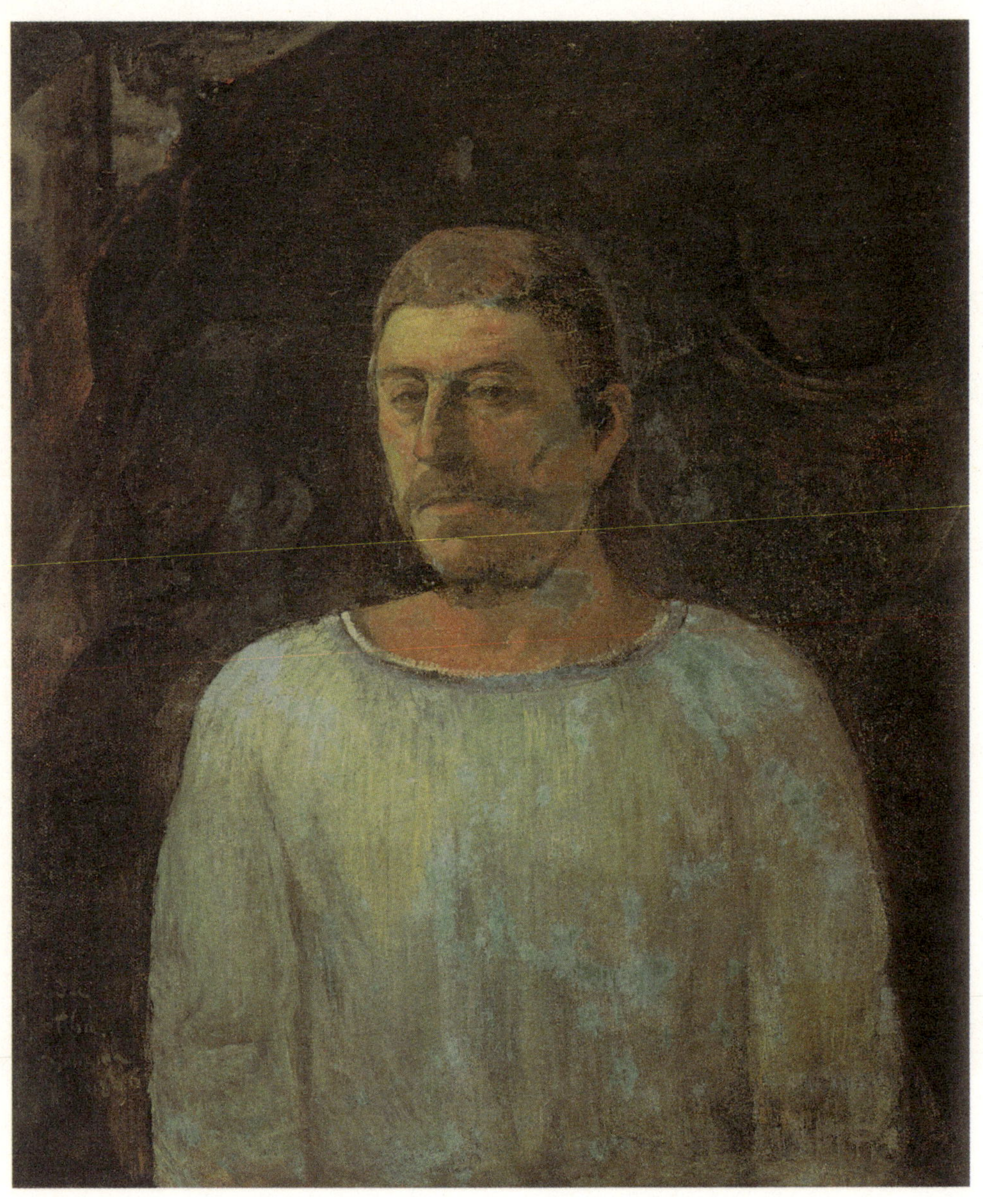

***Self-Portrait Near Golgotha*,**
1896.
Oil on canvas, 76 × 64 cm.
Museu de Arte, São Paulo.

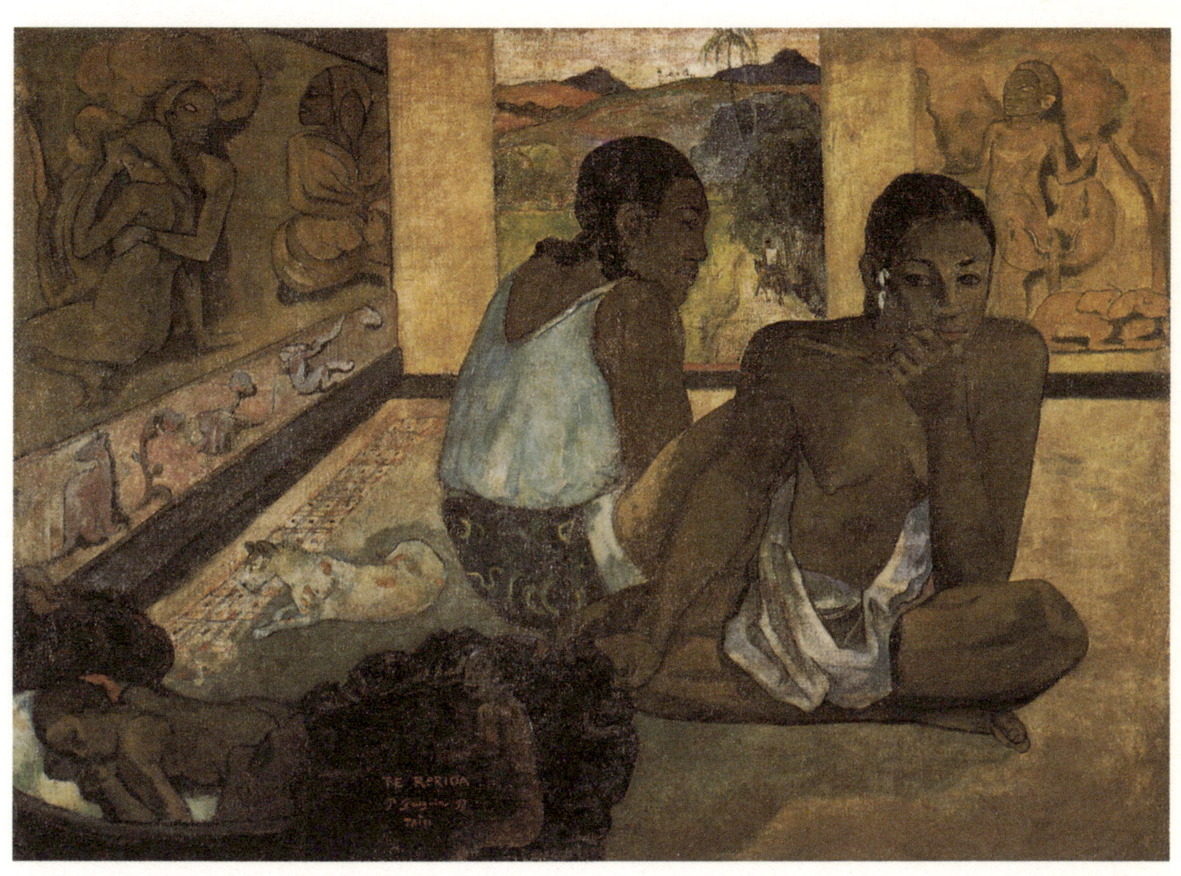

Te Rerioa (The Dream), 1897.
Oil on canvas, 95 × 130 cm.
Courtauld Institute Galleries,
London.

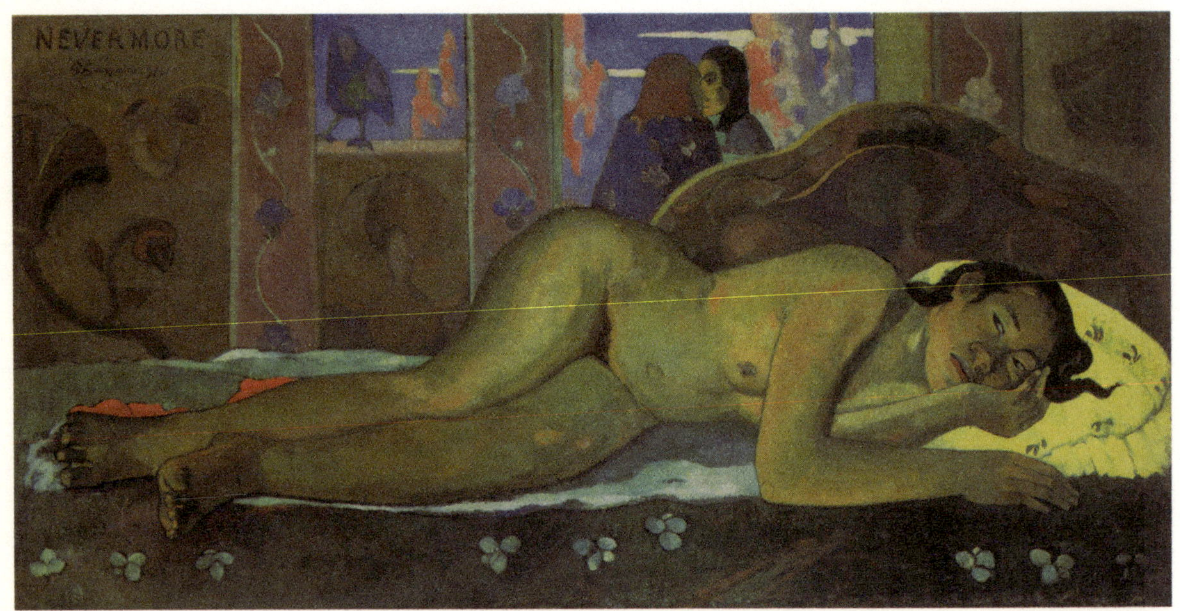

Nevermore, 1897.
Oil on canvas, 60.5 × 116 cm.
Courtauld Institute Galleries,
London.

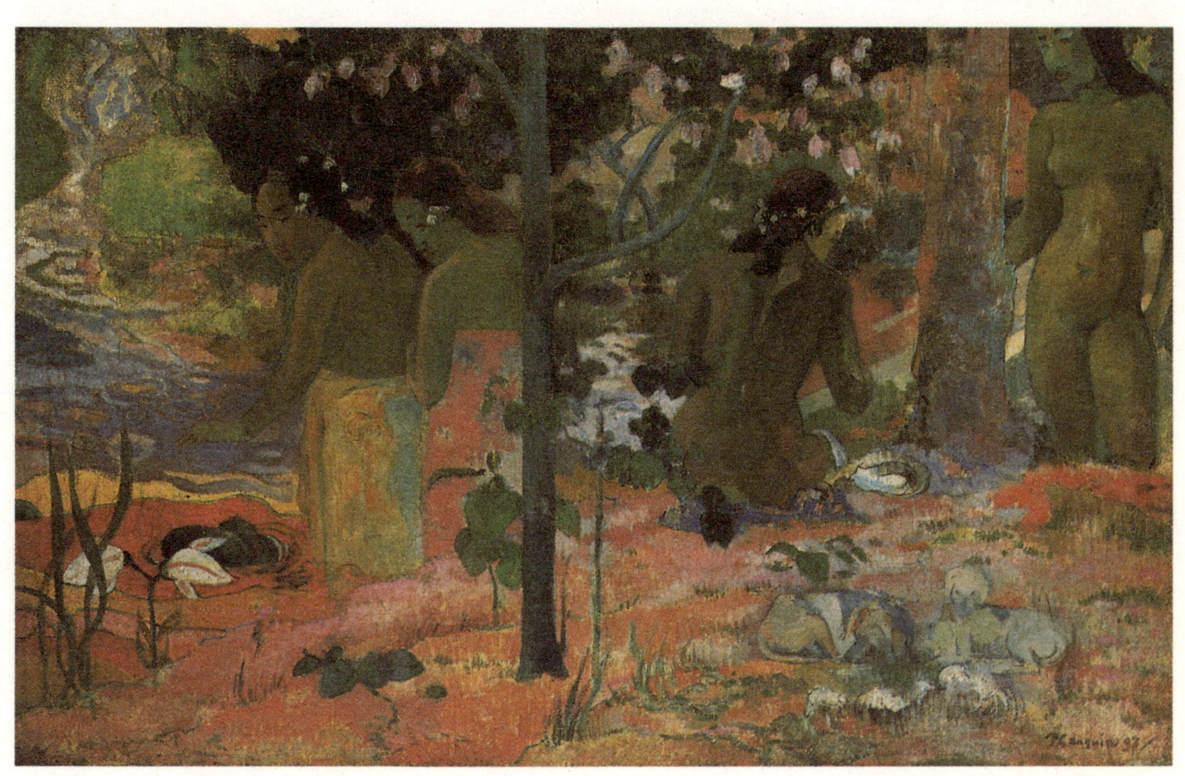

The Bathers, 1897.
Oil on canvas, 60.4 × 93.4 cm.
National Gallery of Art,
Washington.

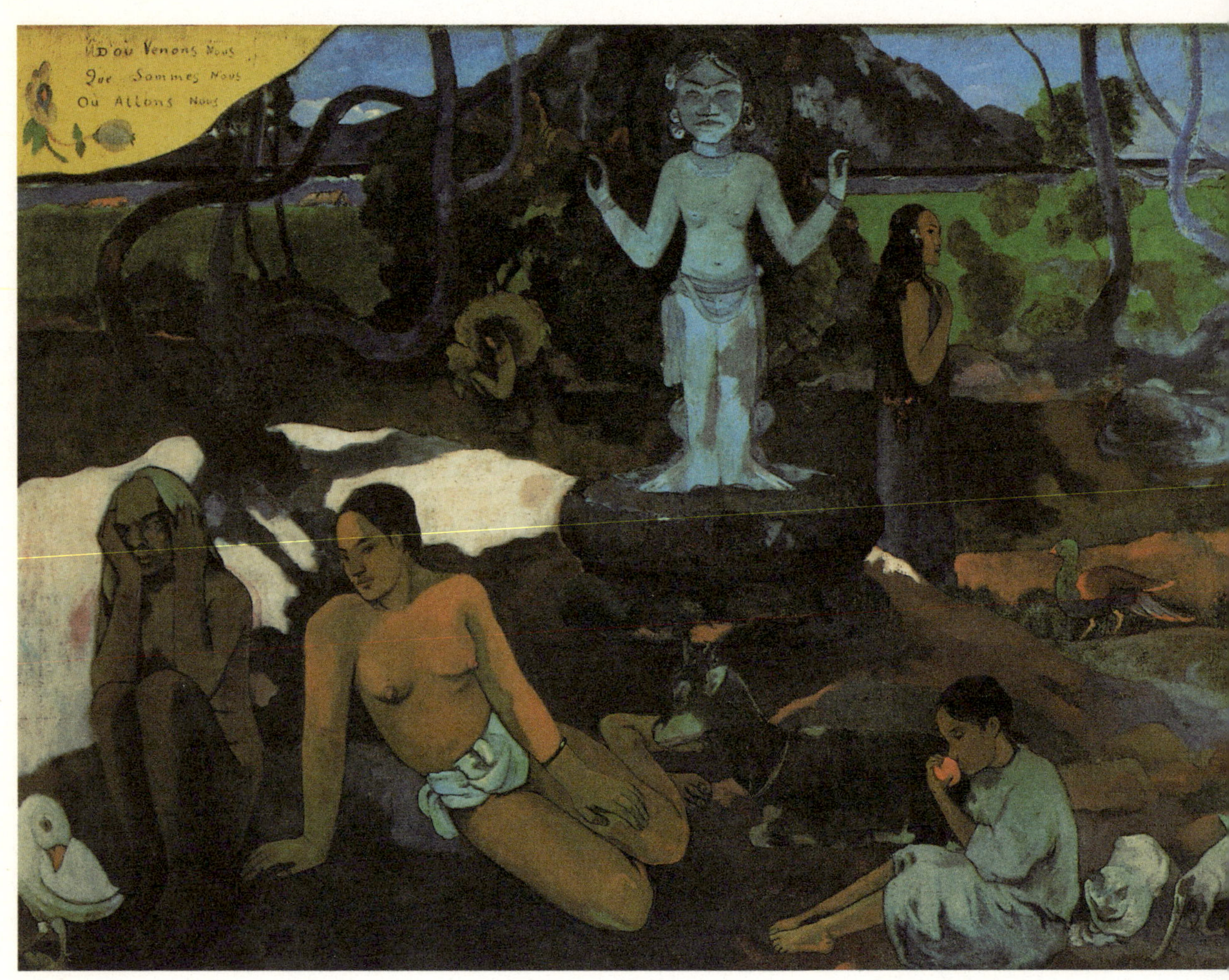

***Where Do We Come From? What Are We? Where Are We Going?*,**
1897.
Oil on canvas, 139.1 × 374.6 cm.
Museum of Fine Arts, Boston.

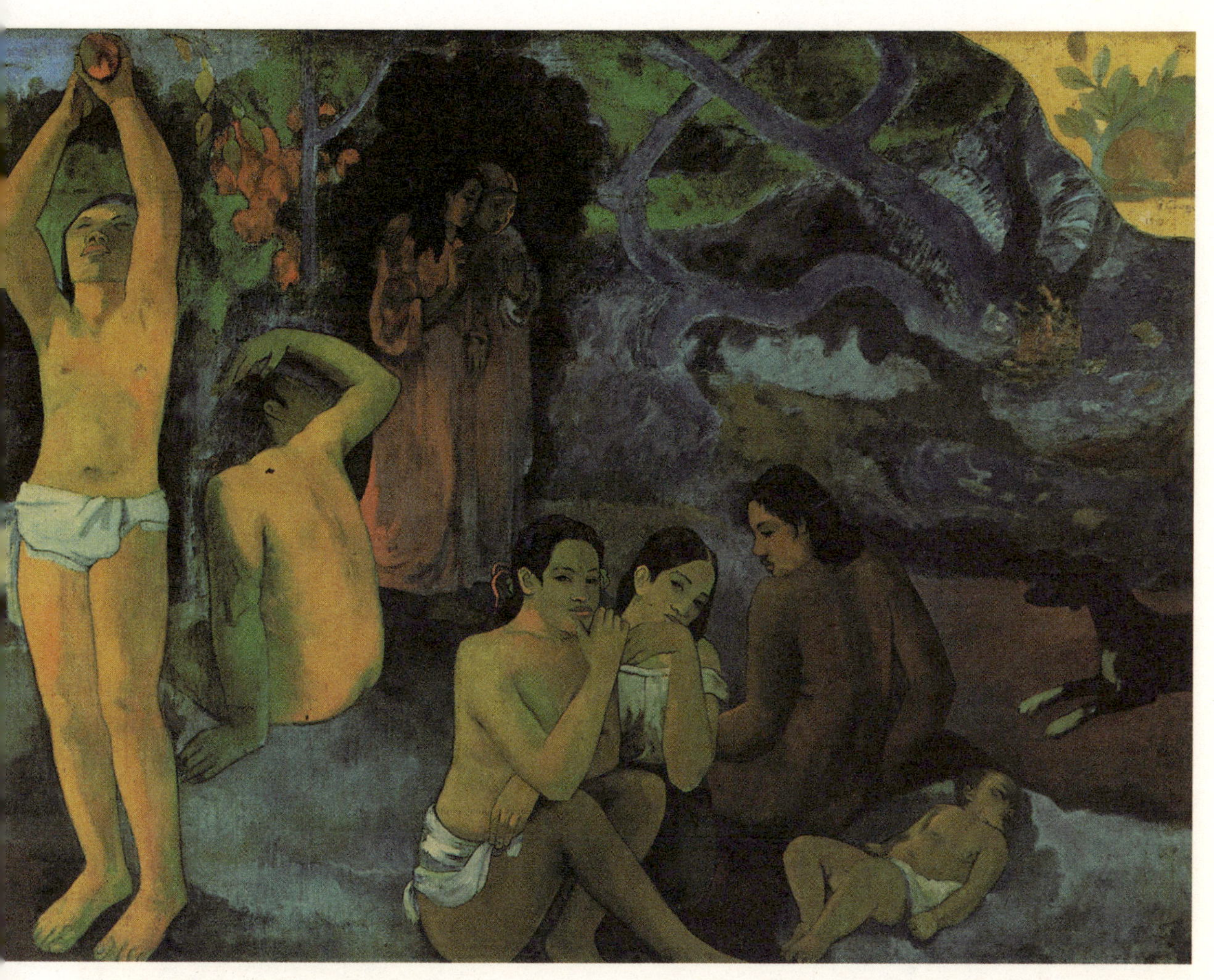

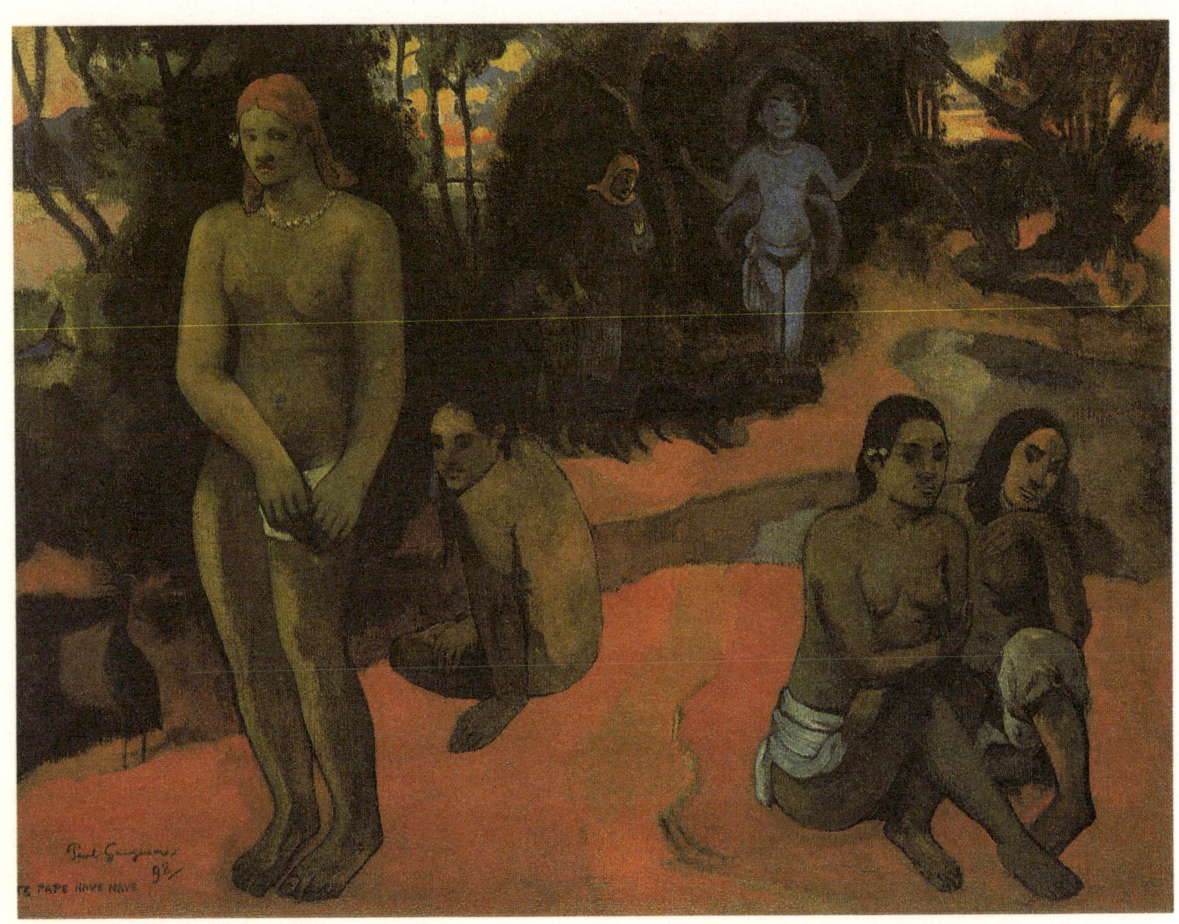

Te pape nave nave (Delectable Waters), 1898.
Oil on canvas, 74 × 95.3 cm.
National Gallery of Art, Washington.

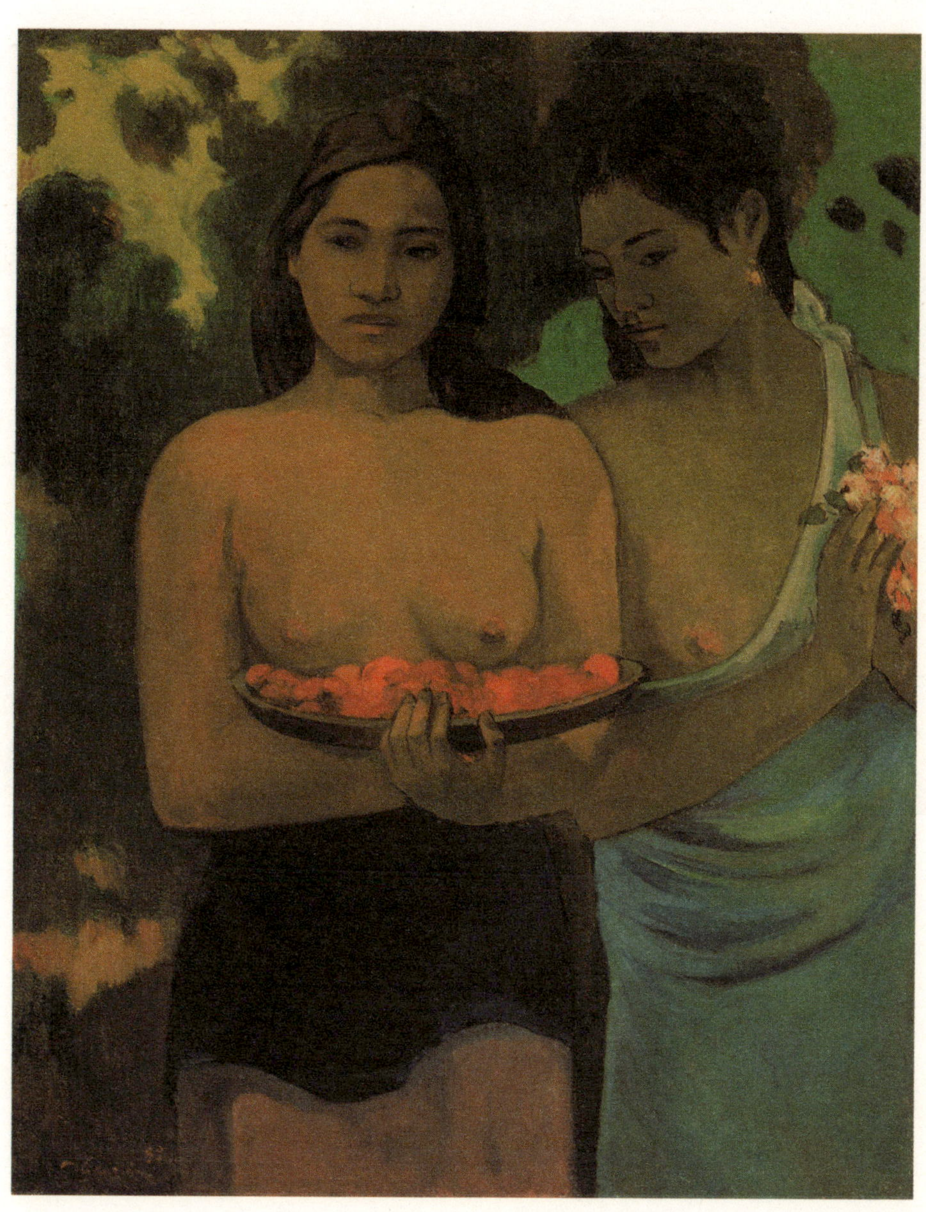

Two Tahitian Women, 1899.
Oil on canvas, 94 × 72.2 cm.
The Metropolitan Museum of
Art, New York.

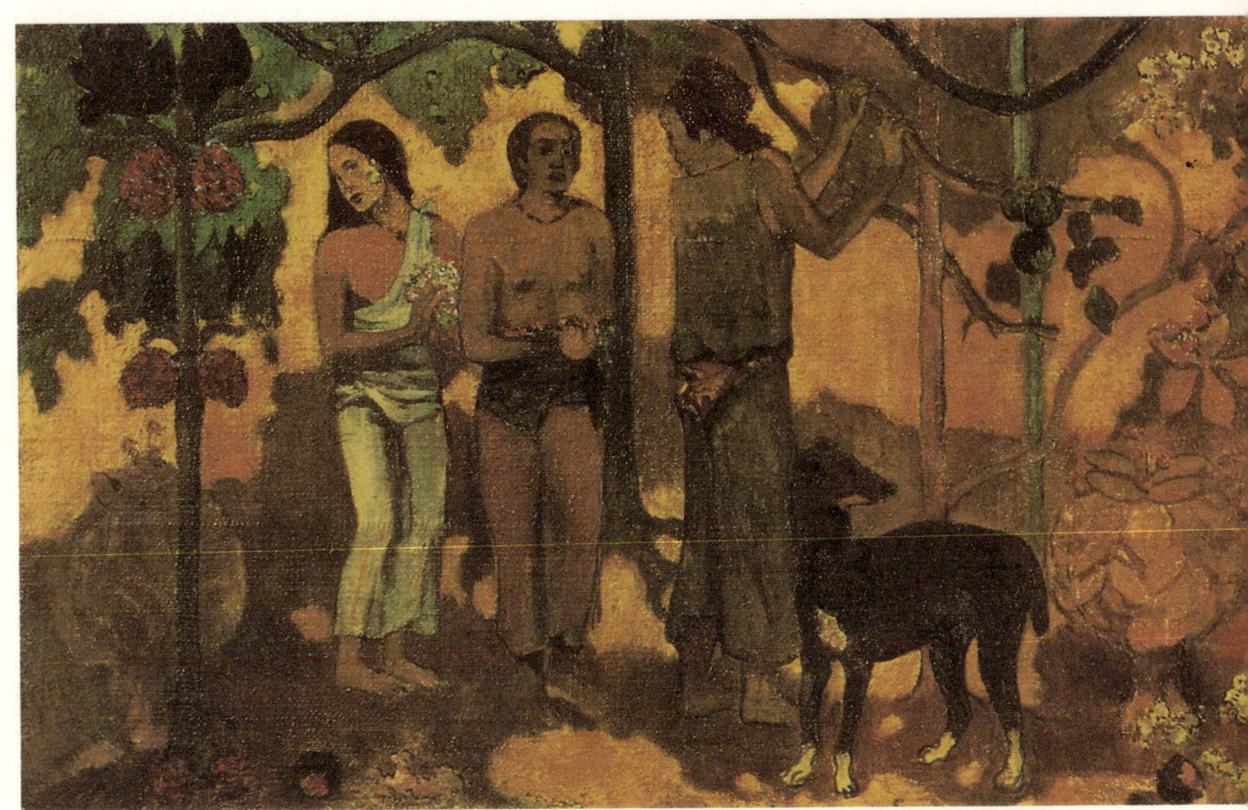

Faa Iheihe (Tahitian Pastoral),
1898.
Oil on canvas, 54 × 169 cm.
Tate Gallery, London.

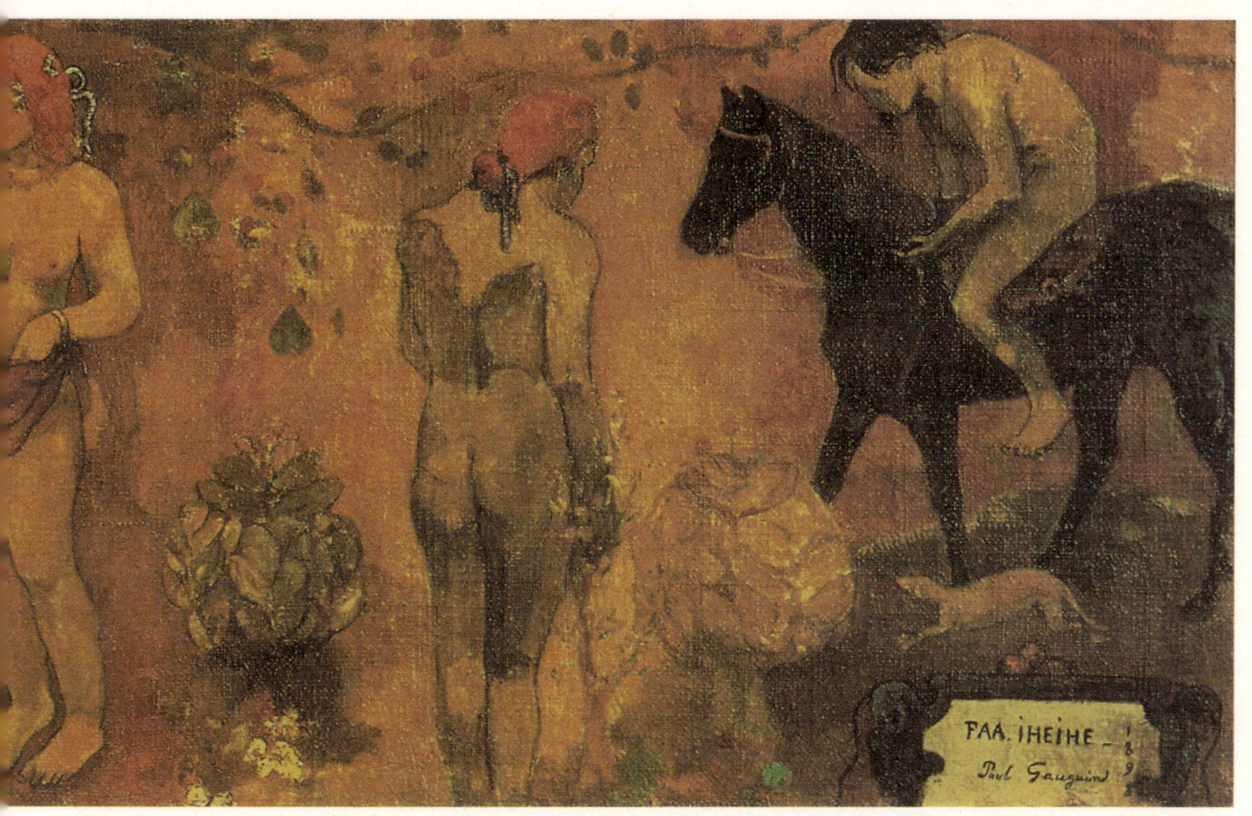
FAA. IHEIHE - 1898
Paul Gauguin

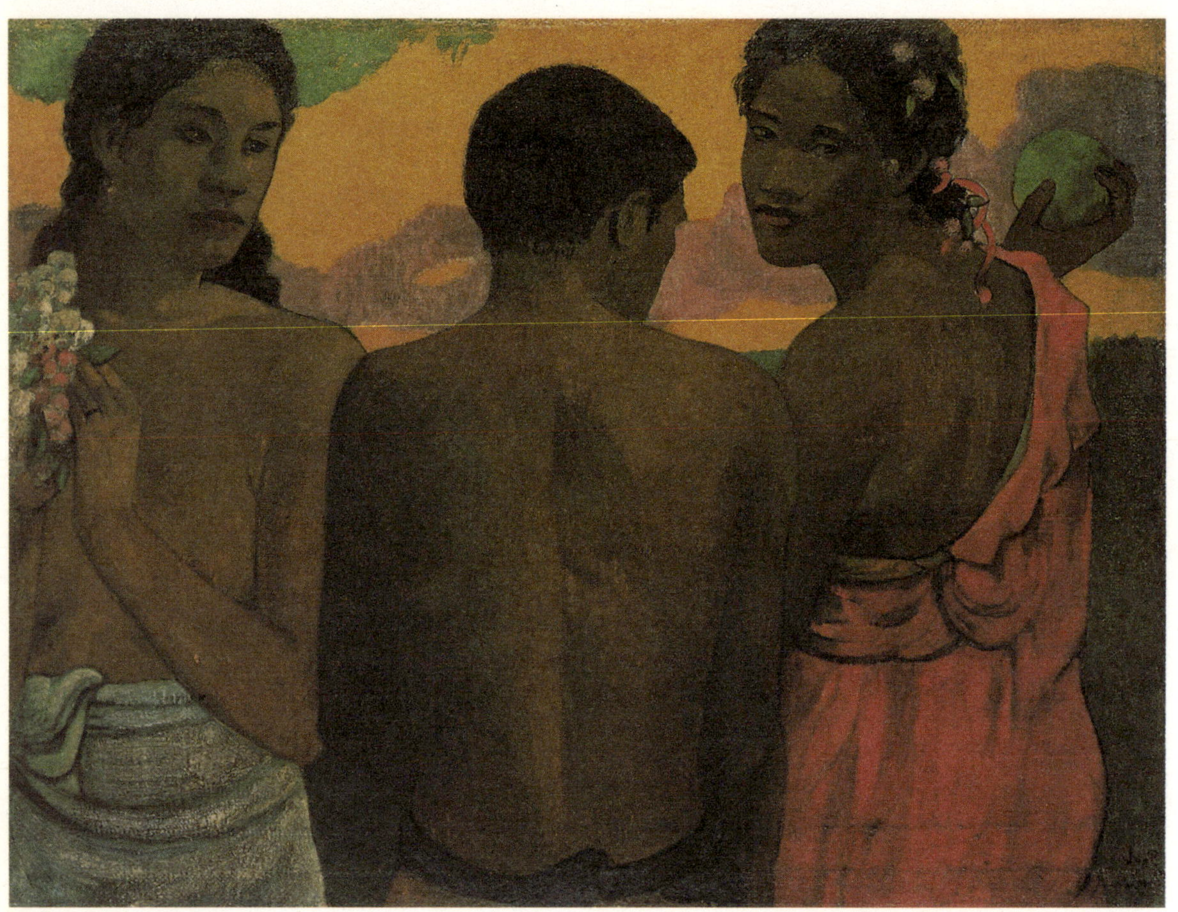

Three Tahitians or Conversation, 1899.
Oil on canvas, 73 × 93 cm.
National Galleries of Scotland, Edinburgh.

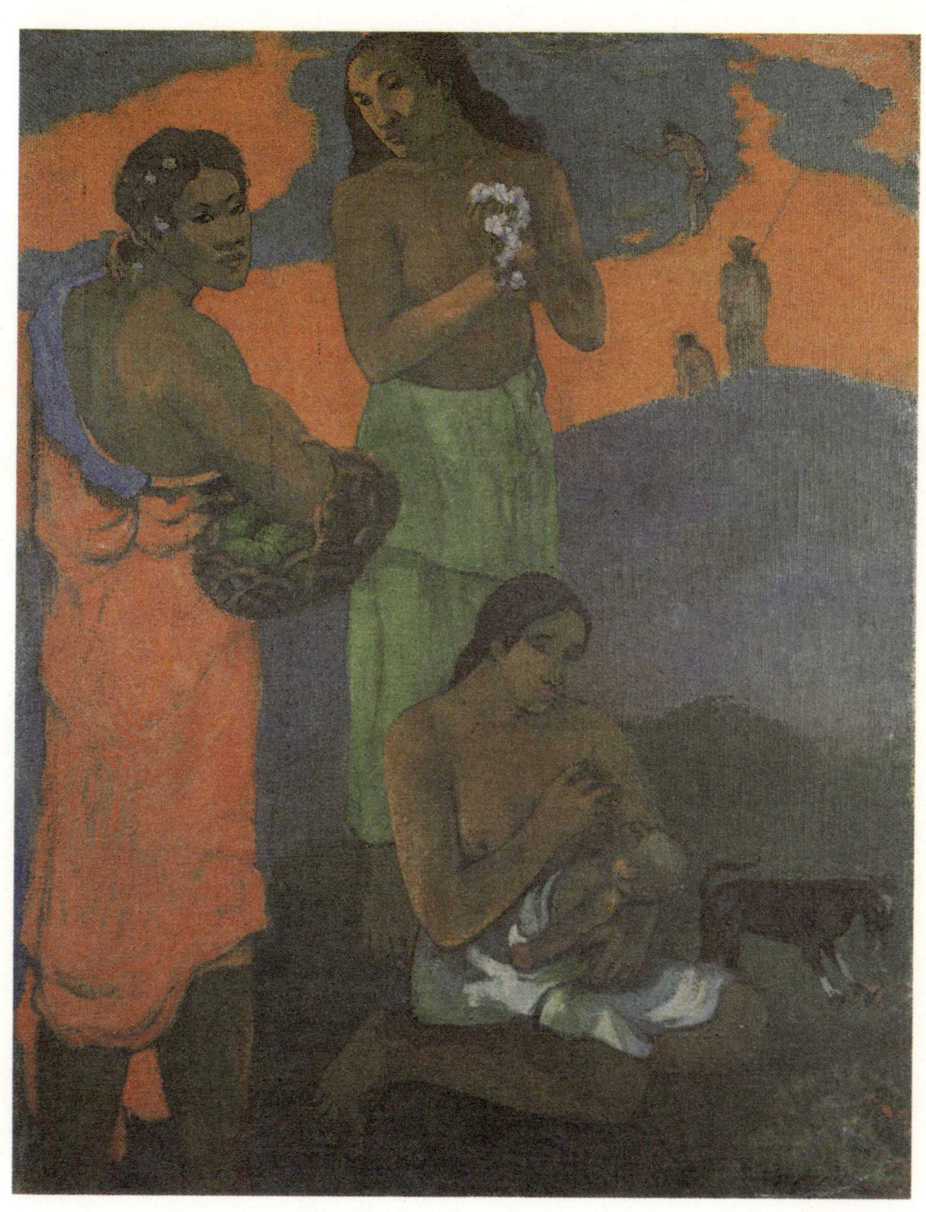

Women on the Seashore or Motherhood, 1899.
Oil on canvas, 95.5 × 73.5 cm.
State Hermitage Museum,
St. Petersburg.

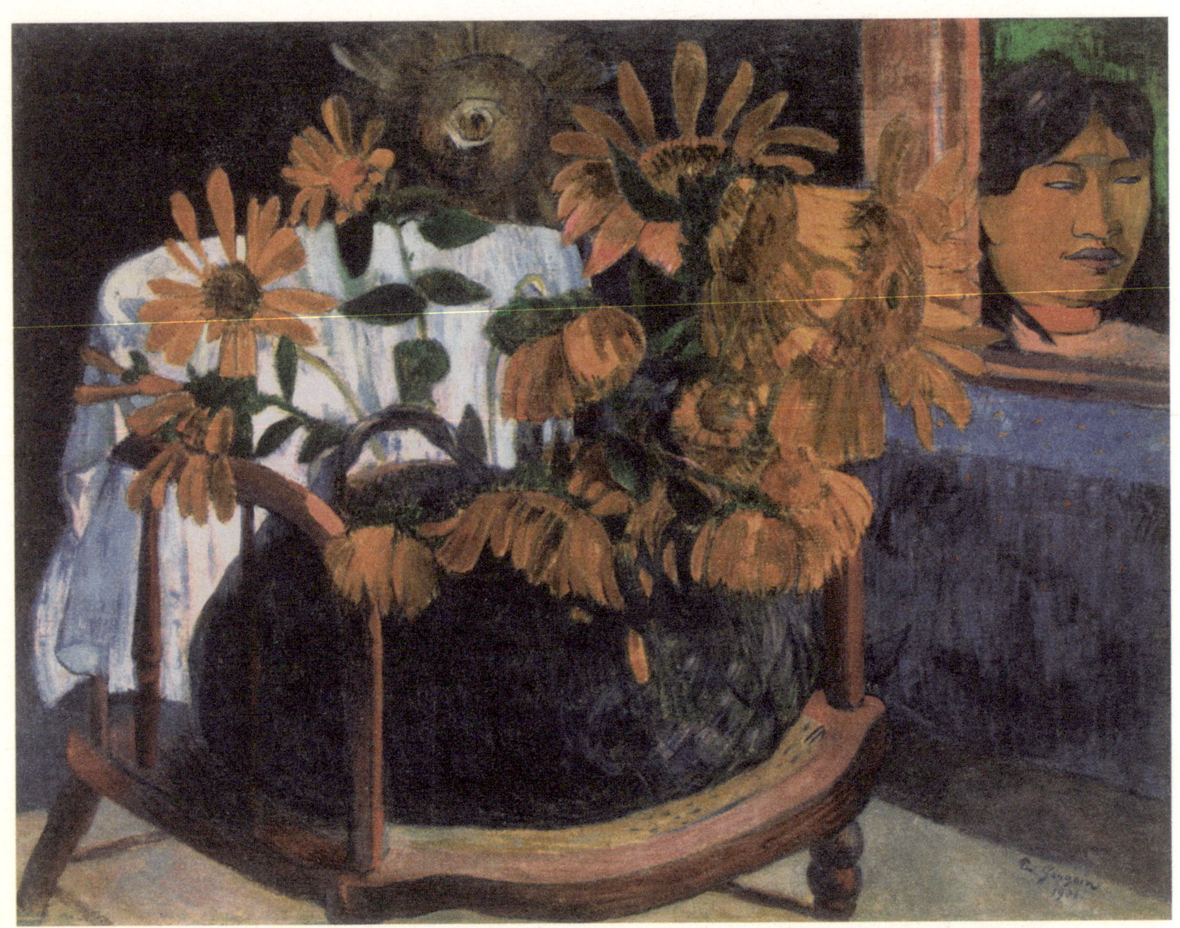

Sunflowers, 1901.
Oil on canvas, 73 × 92.3 cm.
The State Hermitage Museum,
St. Petersburg.

of Pleasure"—just a stone's throw from a police station, a Catholic Church and a Protestant Mission. The house and grounds were themselves works of art, with carved doorjambs and lintels, and other sculpted decoration surrounding the premises. Here he planted a garden with sunflower seeds imported from France, an effort to summon up memories of an earlier time of utopian dreams, when he set up house with Van Gogh in Arles. *The Sunflowers* (1901, p. 84), is an obvious monument to the Dutch artist, known to Gauguin as "the painter of sunflowers." But in addition to its imagery of exuberance and abundance—of Virgil's "ruddy purple," "crocus gold" and "vermillion"—there is the sidelong glance of the woman at the window at right, and the evil eye planted in the middle of a sunflower at top. Even now, amid the delights of the garden, Gauguin recalled the failure of the Arles experiment.

At the House of Pleasure, and generally in the Marquesas, Gauguin positively invited scandal. He displayed pornographic prints, openly pursued liaisons with young native women and wrote and published rumors and obscenities. He was openly flamboyant in his very person, wearing a loosely wrapped *pareu* around his waist and carrying a walking stick whose handle-end was carved into a dildo. He wrote letters of protest to administrators in Tahiti and Paris on any conceivable pretext, sometimes selflessly deploring police brutality toward native people, and at other times senselessly pitching invectives toward colonial officials, or demanding for himself special favors and sinecures. Although in poor health, he undertook to assist Marquesan men and women in their efforts to resist the forced internment of native children in convent schools. "Monsieur Gauguin," wrote Special Corporal Charpillet in a secret communique to the colonial administrator in Papeete, "despite the difficulty he experiences walking, has not hesitated to go by himself to the beach in order to try to convince the natives to remove their children [from the convent boarding schools] and argue that the law cannot oblige parents to send them." His paintings of beach scenes, such as *Riders on the Beach* (1902), reflect this agitated reality. The beach here is not so much a place of pleasure, as an *agora*, where the community may gather to discuss, debate, organize and begin to take action. Similarly, the curious, androgynous figures found in Gauguin's late works, such as *Bathers* (1902) and *Man with a Red Cape* (1902) can be seen as indicators of nascent, anti-colonial struggle; they reveal the artist's growing engagement with a Maohi sexual underground of Mahus (transvestites) and libertines. In April, 1903, just a few weeks before the artist's death, Colonial Inspector Salles reported to the Ministry of the Marine and Colonies in France:

> The Marquesan natives continually indulge in drunken orgies in remote parts of the valleys. On such occasions, groups of forty to fifty persons fill the largest containers in the village with orange wine, and sometimes even use a canoe for the purpose. The men and women, completely nude, will then drink and drink, fight and copulate. The gendarmes know it is very dangerous to arrive in the middle of a feast. The painter Gauguin, who lives in Atuona and defends all the native vices, sees in these savage scenes no more than a simple amusement necessary to the well being of the natives.[17]

Gauguin's ostracism from colonial society and the French state was almost complete; there were even plans to deport him. (There is considerable irony here, since the Marquesas are literally the most remote islands on earth, and a location to which French outlaws and revolutionaries were sometimes exiled!) Yet having set his store in the colonies, Gauguin was determined to remain there until death.

• • •

17 Stephen F. Eisenman, *Gauguin's Skirt*. London: Thames and Hudson, 1997, p. 161.

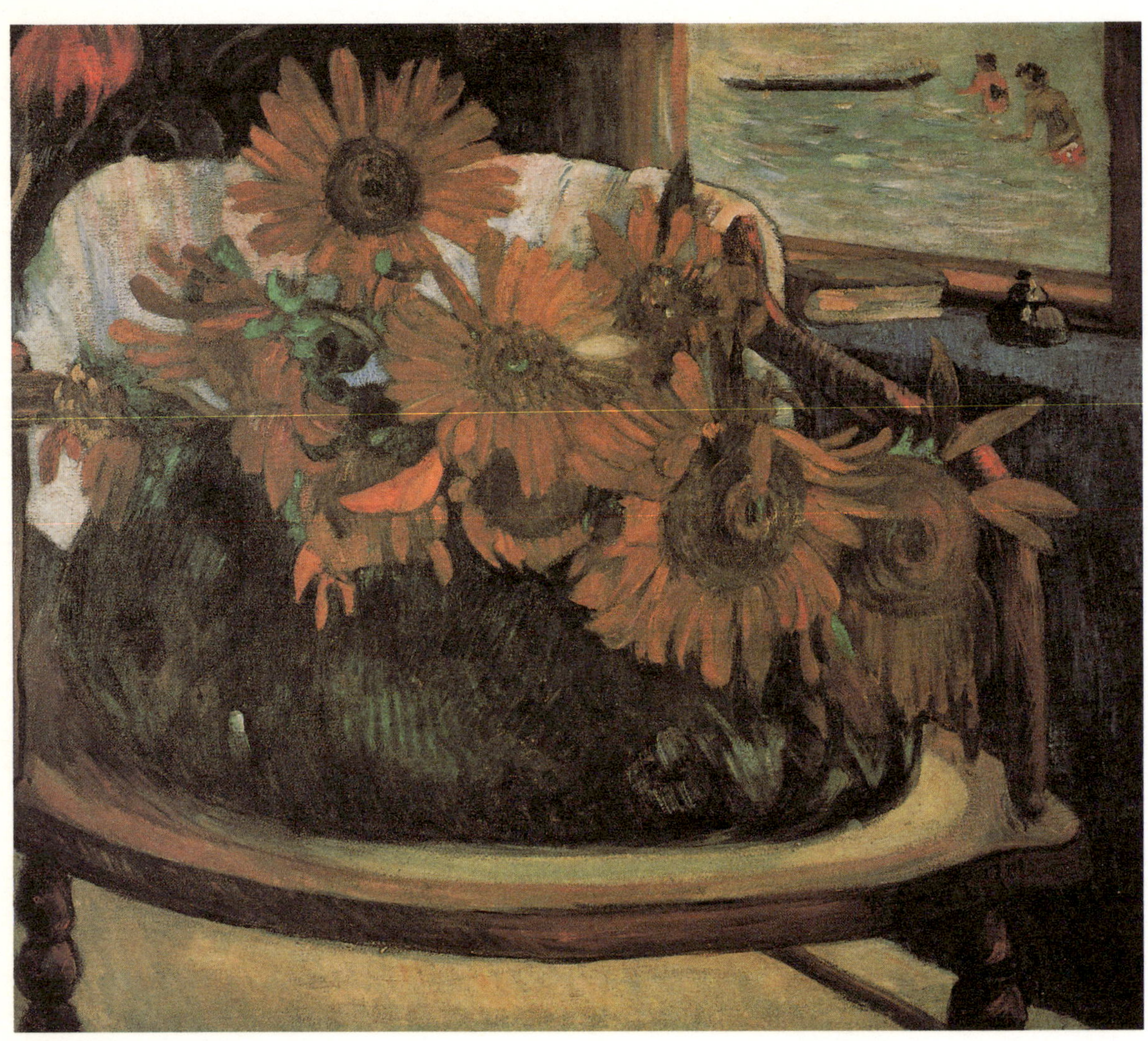

Sunflower on a Chair, 1901.
Oil on canvas, 66 × 75 cm.
Private Collection, Zurich.

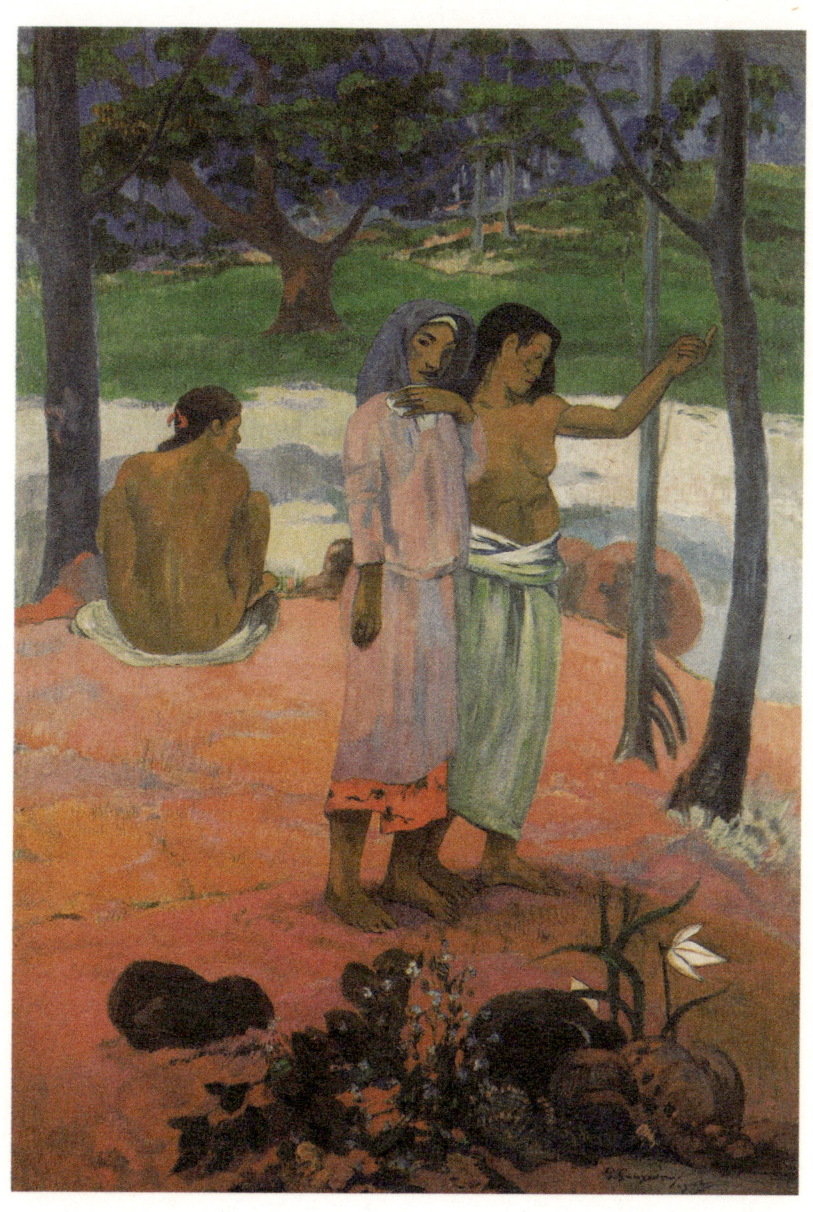

The Call, 1902.
Oil on canvas, 130 × 90 cm.
The Cleveland Museum of Art,
Cleveland.

On May 30, 1903, Monsignor Joseph Martin, vicar of the Marquesas Islands in French Polynesia, issued the following bulletin: "The only recent noteworthy event has been the death of a contemptible individual named Gauguin, a reputed artist, but an enemy of God and everything that is decent." Paul Gauguin died, probably of syphilis, three weeks earlier and was hastily buried in the grounds of Calvary cemetery—represented in the background of *The White Horse* (1902)—overlooking the town of Atuona. A similar landscape is depicted in the placid *Landscape with Pig and Horse* (p. 89) one of the last works of his life, and one which reprises the Golden Age motifs and mythic animals—the fecund agricultural domain of Hesiod's *Works and Days*—that had preoccupied the artist since his Impressionist days. The mourners at Gauguin's funeral were few, and the solemnity of the occasion was marred by a dispute about whether the reprobate artist had wished to be buried in consecrated grounds. In fact, the only ground that would have been suitable, was Arcadia, a distant, golden land the artist never quite reached.

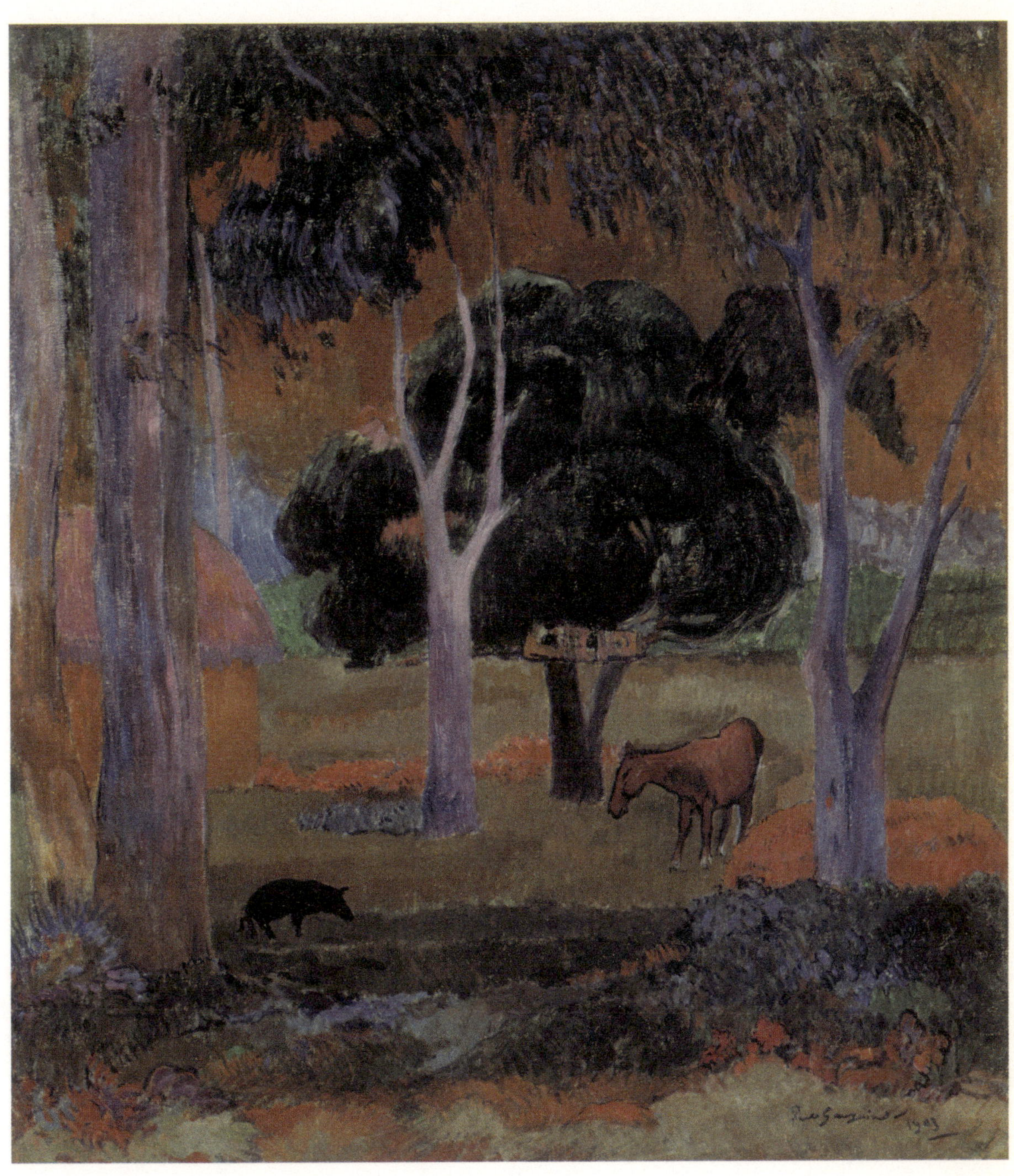

Landscape with Pig and Horse, Hiva OA, 1903.
Oil on canvas, 75 × 67 cm.
Ateneum Art Museum, Helsinki.

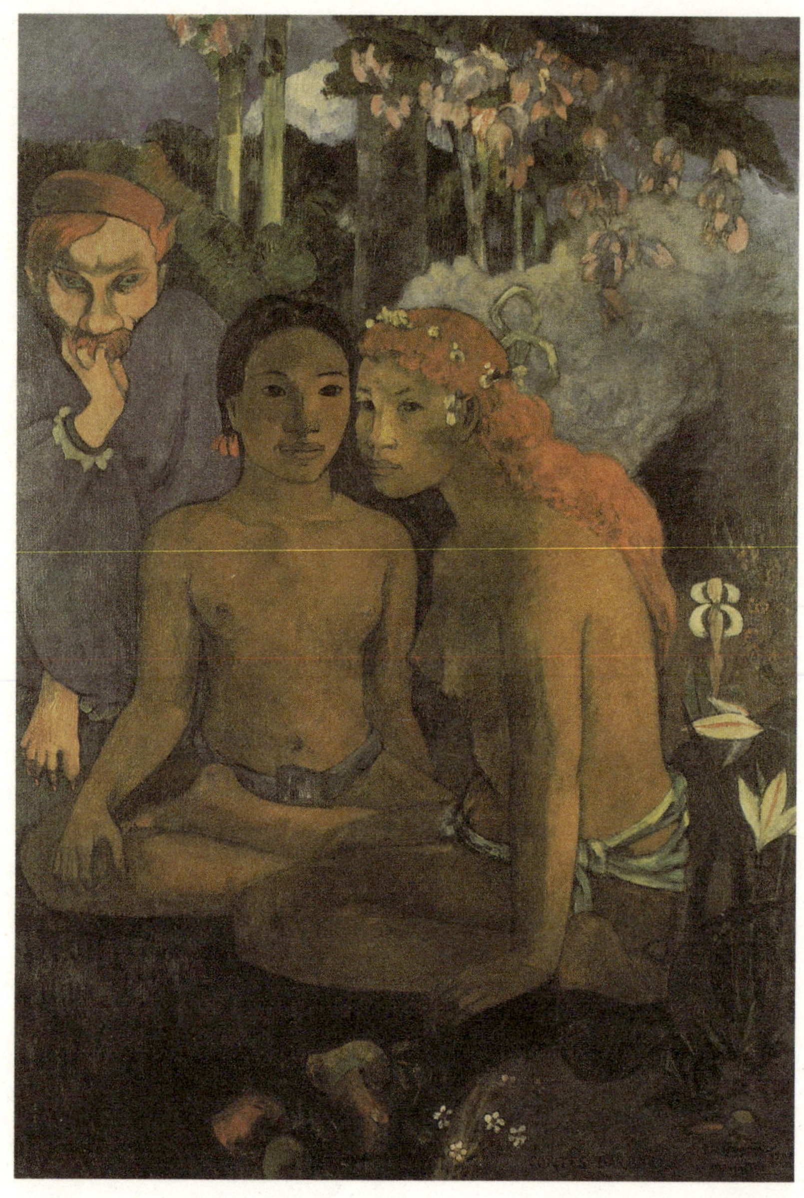

Barbarous Tales, 1902.
Oil on canvas, 131.5 × 90.5 cm.
Museum Folkwang, Essen.

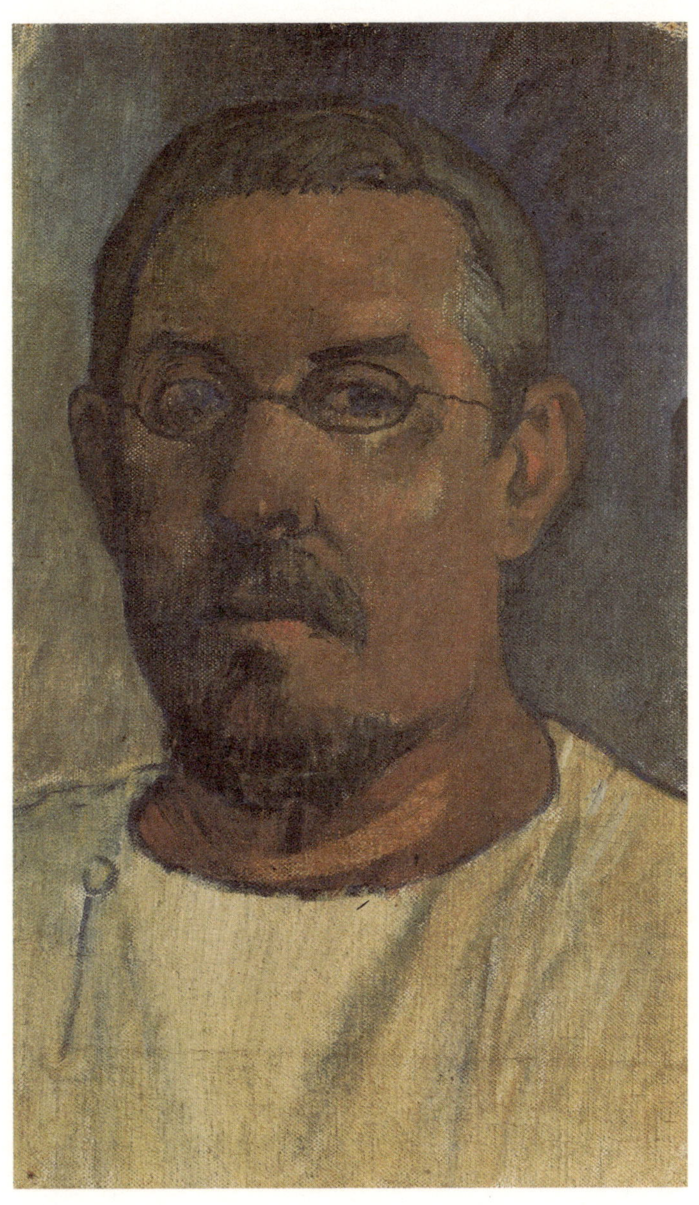

Self-Portrait, c. 1903.
Oil on canvas mounted on wood,
42 × 45 cm.
Kunstmuseum, Basel.

Chronology

1848
Paul Gauguin is born on June 7 in Paris, son to Clovis Gauguin, journalist, and Aline Chazal, descendent of the Viceroy of Peru.

1849
On August 8, the Gauguin family, fearful of the Imperial regime, emigrates to Peru. Paul is only one at the time. Clovis Gauguin dies during the journey.

1851
A coup d'etat is staged by Louis Napoleon, who is named Emperor of the French.

1854-1855
Aline Chazal and her children return to France and settle in Orléans, where Gauguin attends school. He will later further his education at the Saint-Mesmin Chapel seminary.

1864
After studying in Paris and Orléans, he enters the merchant marine. He travels to Rio de Janeiro twice, and circles the globe.

1867
On a stopover in India on his way to Rio de Janeiro, he learns of the death of his mother.

1872
He leaves the merchant marine and begins to work as a stockbroker, a lucrative position that he gets thanks to Gustave Arosa.

1873
He works as a stockbroker and lives with his wife Mette Gad. He paints in his free time.

1874-1875
He becomes increasingly involved in the avant-garde art scene. He meets Camille Pisarro, a friend of Arosa, who becomes his teacher and mentor. Pisarro recommends that he collect Impressionist paintings.

1876
He is accepted by the Official Salon and exhibits his landscape *In the Forest Viroflay*.

1877
He learns new sculptural techniques from Jukes Bouillot.

1878-80
He works in order to support his painting. At the invitation of Pissarro and Degas, he exhibits his work along with Impressionists. He is drawn to the novelist and critic Joris-Karl Huysmans.

The book *The Marriage of Loti* by Pierre Loti (Julien Viaud) is published. It attracts the interest of both Gauguin and Van Gogh.

1881
He sells three works to Durand-Ruelm, an art dealer and patron of Impressionism.

1882
With the drop in the French financial markets, he loses a good deal of his assets as well as his job.

1884
He moves to Denmark, where his wife was born, to save money as well as his art collection.

1885
He exhibits his work at the Society of the Friends of Art and questions the failure of the press to give the event greater coverage. He believes that the exhibition was obscured by the influence of the "old academic clan."

1886
He shows nineteen paintings and a woodcut at the eighth Impressionist exhibition. He sells a painting to artist Felix Bracquemond. He meets Vincent van Gogh for the first time. Meanwhile, he openly breaks with the neo-Impressionist movement.

1887
He leaves for Panama with his friend Charles Laval. For two months, he works on the construction of the Panama Canal, but he cannot continue due to tropical diseases. When he recovers, he continues his journey to Martinique, but he only stays there briefly: he decides to return to France because of his delicate health. This brief stay in the Caribbean, though, proves crucial to his later work. It teaches him about the sensuality of color and he becomes interested in primitive nature capable of accentuating human relations.

1888
Theo van Gogh offers to help him financially. The proposal entails moving to Arles with Vincent Van Gogh. He agrees to work with Van Gogh, though their brief experience together is turbulent. Vincent van Gogh threatens Gauguin with a razor blade and then cuts off a piece of his ear.

He and Bernard work on a treatise that distances them from Impressionism. Synthetist theory maintains that artist creation must synthesize the external and formal appearance of the subject, the artist's feelings and the formal composition of the work in its entirety.

1889
He exhibits "Les XX" in Brussels, though these twenty works are not well received. He

returns to Paris to work on an exhibition of Impressionist painters who are rejected by the jury of the World's Fair. He takes part in the exhibition at the Café des Arts, also known as Café Volpini. Fellow participants in that show include artists who later become known as the "Pont-Aven School," which rejects Impressionism and Realism in favor of Synthetism, a style characterized by a simplification of forms and colors.

1890
He applies for a job in Tonkin, a French protectorate in Southeast Asia. He dreams of traveling to Madagascar.

1891
He becomes close to the literary circle associated with Symbolism. He frequents the studio of Bonard, Denis and Viullard. He travels to Tahiti, where he founds what he calls the "Studio of the Tropics". He and his Anglo-Tahitian lover move to Mataiea, where he rents a cabin to work with native models.

1892
He is hospitalized in Papeete after suffering a hemorrhage. He does not pursue treatment due to the expense. He recovers and receives the news that in a publication Aurier Further has credited him with having created the Symbolist movement.

1893
He leaves Tahiti for France. He takes with him sixty-six paintings and a good many sculptures which he offers to the collector and painter Daniel de Monfreid. A few days after arriving in France, he travels to Marseilles to attend the funeral of his aunt Isadore, who leaves him 13,000 francs. He starts working on a book to provide a context for his work in Tahiti.

1894
Morice and other friends pay him tribute. He holds a week-long exhibition in his studio, at which he announces his return to Tahiti because he prefers the wild world of the island to life in Paris.

1895
He leaves Marseilles for Tahiti. There are several stopovers along the way, and he has the opportunity to visit Sydney, Auckland and New Zealand, where he studies Maori art.

1896
Desperate, he writes to Morice and tells him that he is suffering from pains in his leg, as well as depression and poverty. He asks Morice to buy two of his Van Gogh paintings.

1897
He has several art attacks and is bedridden.

1898
In a letter to his friend Daniel de Monfreid, he explains that his new "large painting" , later known as *D'où venos nous?* has been on his mind since his failed suicide attempt. One month later, he says that he is working like the devil to finish the piece.

1900
He reaches an agreement with Vollard whereby he will produce between twenty and twenty-four paintings a year in exchange for a monthly salary.

1901
He is hospitalized three times. He receives an advance on his yearly stipend from Vollard and plans to move to the Marquesas Islands in search of a simple life. He moves to his new home, which he calls "the House of Pleasures."

1902
He begins a prolific period during which he finishes more than thirty pieces and works on his manuscript *The Modern Spirit and Catholicism*. He suffers eczema, which prevents him from painting. He works on writing *Avant et Après.*

1903
He grows very ill from syphilis and dies on May 9.

Bibliography

PAUL GAUGUIN'S WRITINGS (MAIN EDITIONS)

À ma fille Aline, ce cahier est dédié. Bourdeaux: Ed. facsimile, 1989.

Ancien culte mahori. René Huyghe (ed.). Paris: La Palme, 1951.

Avant et après. Paris: Ed. facsimile, 1994.

Cahier pour Aline. S. Damiron (ed.). Paris: Ed. facsimile, 1963.

Carnet de Tahiti. Bernard Dorival (ed.). Paris: Ed. facsimile, 1954.

Correspondence de Paul Gauguin. Victor Merlhès (ed.). Paris: Fondation Singer-Polignac, 1984.

Gauguin e Tahiti-Noa Noa. Mirella Tenderini (ed.). Turin: CDA & Vivalda, 2005.

Lettres de Gauguin à André Fontainas. André Fontainas (intr.). Paris: Ed. facsimile, 1929.

Lettres de Gauguin à sa femme et à ses amis. Maurice Malingue (ed.). Paris: Grasset, 1946; Cleveland and New York, 1949.

Lettres de Gauguin, Gide, Huysmans, Jammes, Mallarmé, Verhaeren [...] à Odilon Redon. Roseline Bacou, and Ari Redon (eds.). Paris: José Corti, 1960.

Lettres de Paul Gauguin à Georges-Daniel de Monfreid. A. Joly-Segalen (ed.). Paris: Ed. facsimile, 1918; ed. rev., 1950.

Lettres de Paul Gauguin à Émile Bernard. 1888-1891. Geneva: Pierre Gailler, 1954.

Lettres de Vincent van Gogh, Paul Gauguin, Odilon Redon, Paul Cézanne, Élémir Bourges, Leon Bloy, Guillaume Apollinaire, Joris-Karl Huysmans, Henry de Groux à Émile Bernard. Brussels: Éditions de la Nouvelle revue Belgique, 1942.

Noa Noa. Pierre Petit (ed.). Paris: Ed. facsimile, 1988; New York, 1985.

Oviri. Ecrits d'un sauvage. Daniel Guérin (ed.). Paris: Gallimard, 1974.

Paul Gauguin. Letters to Ambroise Vollard and André Fontainas. John Rewald (ed.). San Francisco: The Grabhorn Press, 1943.

CATALOGUES RAISONNÉS

Bodelsen, Merete. *Gauguin's Ceramics. A Study in the Development of His Art.* London: Faber & Faber, 1964.

Field, Richard. *Paul Gauguin. Monotypes.* Philadelphia: Philadelphia Museum of Art, 1973.

Gray, Christopher. *Sculpture and Ceramics of Paul Gauguin.* Baltimore: John Hopkins Press, 1963.

Guérin, Marcel. *L'oeuvre gravé de Gauguin.* Paris: H. Fleury, 1927; rev. ed., San Francisco, 1980.

Mongan, Elizabeth; Eberhard W. Kornfeld, and Harold Joachin. *Paul Gauguin. Catalogue Raisonné of His Prints.* Bern: Galerie Kornfeld, 1988.

Wildenstein, Georges; Raymond Cogniat, and Daniel Wildenstein. *Gauguin. Catalogue. L'art français.* Vol. 1. Paris: Les Beaux-Arts, 1964.

Wildenstein, Georges; Sylvie Crussard, and Martine Heudron. *Gauguin. A Savage in the Making. Catalogue Raisonné of the Paintings (1873-1888).* 2 vols. Milan and Paris: Skira, 2002.

Zingg, Jean-Pierre. *Les éventails de Paul Gauguin.* Paris: Editions Avant & Apres, 1996.

STUDIES AND EXHIBITION CATALOGUES

Alexandre, Arsène. *Paul Gauguin. Sa vie et le sens de son oeuvre.* Paris: Bernheim-Jeune, 1930.

Andersen, Wayne V. *Gauguin's Paradise Lost.* New York: Viking Press, 1971.

Bessanova, Marina et al. *Impressionists and Post Impressionists in Soviet Museums.* Leningrad: Phaidon, 1985.

Boudaille, Georges. *Gauguin.* 1st ed. Paris: Somogy, 1963; London, 1964.

Brettell, Richard R., and Anne-Birgitte Fonsmark. *Gauguin and Impressionism.* New Haven and London: Yale University Press, 2005.

Cachin, Françoise. *Gauguin.* Paris: Flammarion, 1968; reed., 1988.

Catalog for the Exhibition Gauguin. Paris: Grand Palais, 1989.

Chassé, Charles. *Gauguin et son temps.* Paris: La Bibliotheque des Arts, 1955.

Cogniat, Raymond, and John Rewald. *Paul Gauguin. A Sketchbook.* Paris and New York: Ed. facsimile, 1962.

Cooper, Douglas (ed.). *Paul Gauguin. 45 lettres à Vincent, Théo, et Jo van Gogh.* The Hague and Lausanne: Ed. facsimile, 1983.

Danielsson, Bengt. *Love in the South Seas.* London: Allen & Unwin, 1956.

Dorival, Bernard. "Le Milieu," in: *Gauguin.* Paris: Flammarion, 1960; Paris, 1961; Paris, 1986.

Dorra, Henri. *The Symbolism of Paul Gauguin. Erotica, Exotica, and the Great Dilemmas of Humanity.* Berkeley: University of California, 2007.

Edmond, Rod. *Representing the South Pacific. Colonial Discourse from Cook to Gauguin.* Cambridge: Cambridge University Press, 1997.

Eisenman, Stephen F. *Gauguin's Skirt.* London: Thames and Hudson, 1997.

Eisenman, Stephen F. (ed.). *Paul Gauguin. Artist of Myth and Dream.* Milan: Skira Editore, 2007.

Fénéon, Félix. "Calendrier de décembre 1887. Vitrines des marchands de tableaux," in: *La Revue indépendante,* 1888. Included in: Félix Fénéon, *Oeuvres plus que complètes.* Joan U. Halperin (ed.). Vol. 1. Geneva: Droz, 1970, pp. 90-91.

Field, Richard. *Paul Gauguin. The Painting of the First Voyage to Tahiti.* New York: Garland, 1977.

Fonsmark, Anne-Birgitte. *Gauguin Ceramics.* Copenhagen: Ny Carlsberg Glyptotek, 1986.

Gauguin. Actes du Colloque Gauguin. Exhibition catalogue. Paris: Musée d'Orsay, 1991.

Gauguin Drawings. New York / London: Yoseloff, 1958.

Gauguin in the South Seas. London: Allen and Unwin, 1965; New York, 1966.

Gauguin, Pola. *My Father, Paul Gauguin.* New York: Wolfenden Press, 1937.

Guérin, Daniel (ed.). *The Writings of a Savage. Paul Gauguin.* New York: Viking Press, 1978.

Hoog, Michel. *Paul Gauguin. Life and Work.* New York: Rizolli, 1987.

Huyghe, René. *Paul Gauguin.* Paris: Hachette, 1959; Paris, 1967.

Huysmans, Joris-Karl. "L'exposition des indépendants en 1881," in: *L'Art moderne.* Paris: Charpentier, 1883, pp. 85-123.

Kane, William M. "Gauguin's Cheval Blanc. Sources and Syncretic Meanings," in: *The Burlington Magazine,* 180 (760), July 1966, p. 356.

La Faille, J.B. de. *The Works of Vincent van Gogh. His Paintings and Drawings.* New York: Reynal & Company, 1970.

Le Pichon, Yann. *Sur les traces de Gauguin.* Paris: Robert Laffont, 1986; New York, 1986.

Malingue, Maurice. *Gauguin, le peintre et son oeuvre.* Paris: Les Presses de la Cité, 1943; Paris, 1948.

Maugham, Somerset. *A Writer's Notebook.* London: Heinemann, 1949.

Mauner, Georges. *The Nabis. Their History, Their Art 1886-1896.* New York: Garland Publishing, 1978.

Merlhès, Victor (ed.). *Racontars de rapin.* Paris: Editions Avant & Après, 2002.

Paul Gauguin. Paris, 1889. Cleveland: The Cleveland Museum of Art, 2009.

Perruchot, Henri. *La vie de Gauguin.* Paris: Hachette, 1961.

Pickvance, Ronald. *The Drawings of Gauguin.* New York: Hamlyn, 1970.

"Review of *Correspondance de Paul Gauguin: Tome Premier, 1873-1888.* Ed. Victor Merlhès," *Burlington Magazine,* 127 (987), June 1985, pp. 394-395.

Rey, Robert. *Onze menus de Paul Gauguin.* Geneva: G. Cramer, 1950.

Rewald, John. *Gauguin.* Paris: Hyperion, 1938.

Rosskill, Mark. *Van Gogh, Gauguin, and the Impressionist Circle.* Connecticut: Graphic Society , 1970.

Segalen, Victor. "Hommage à Gauguin," in: *Lettres de Paul Gauguin à Georges-Daniel de Monfreid.* Paris: Editions Georges Crès, 1918, pp. 1-77; rev. ed., Paris, 1950, pp. 11-47.

Silverman, Debora. *Van Gogh and Gauguin. The Search for Sacred Art.* New York: Paperback, 2000.

Solana, Guillermo. "The Faun Awakes. Gauguin and the Revival of the Pastoral," in: *Gauguin and the Origins of Symbolism.* Madrid: Fundación Colección Thyssen-Bornemisza, 2005.

"Un lettre inédite de Gauguin," in: *Les Marges,* vol. 14, May 1918, pp. 168-169.

Van Gogh, Vincent. *Correspondance complete de Vincent van Gogh.* 3 vols. Paris: Gallimard, 1960; Boston, 1978.